DISCIPLINARY LITERACY IN PRIMARY SCHOOLS

READING, WRITING AND SPEAKING ACROSS THE CURRICULUM

SHAREEN WILKINSON

Together we unlock every learner's unique potential

At Hachette Learning (formerly Hodder Education), there's one thing we're certain about. No two students learn the same way. That's why our approach to teaching begins by recognising the needs of individuals first.

Our mission is to allow every learner to fulfil their unique potential by empowering those who teach them. From our expert teaching and learning resources to our digital educational tools that make learning easier and more accessible for all, we provide solutions designed to maximise the impact of learning for every teacher, parent and student.

Aligned to our parent company, Hachette Livre, founded in 1826, we pride ourselves on being a learning solutions provider with a global footprint.

www.hachettelearning.com

Although every effort has been made to ensure that website addresses are correct at time of going to press, Hachette Learning cannot be held responsible for the content of any website mentioned in this book. It is sometimes possible to find a relocated web page by typing in the address of the home page for a website in the URL window of your browser.

Hachette UK's policy is to use papers that are natural, renewable and recyclable products and made from wood grown in well-managed forests and other controlled sources. The logging and manufacturing processes are expected to conform to the environmental regulations of the country of origin.

To order, please visit www.HachetteLearning.com or contact Customer Service at education@hachette.co.uk / +44 (0)1235 827827.

ISBN: 978 1 0360 0630 3

© Shareen Wilkinson 2025

First published in 2025 by
Hachette Learning,
An Hachette UK Company
Carmelite House
50 Victoria Embankment
London EC4Y 0DZ
www.HachetteLearning.com

The authorised representative in the EEA is Hachette Ireland, 8 Castlecourt Centre, Dublin 15, D15 XTP3, Ireland (email: info@hbgi.ie)

Impression number   10 9 8 7 6 5 4 3 2 1
Year   2029 2028 2027 2026 2025

All rights reserved. Apart from any use permitted under UK copyright law, no part of this publication may be reproduced or transmitted in any form or by any means, electronic or mechanical, including photocopying and recording, or held within any information storage and retrieval system, without permission in writing from the publisher or under licence from the Copyright Licensing Agency Limited. Further details of such licences (for reprographic reproduction) may be obtained from the Copyright Licensing Agency Limited, www.cla.co.uk

Cover image: Shutterstock: Siberian Art, Natalie Osipova
Illustrations by DC Graphic Design Limited, Hextable, Kent.
Typeset in the UK.
Printed in the UK.
A catalogue record for this title is available from the British Library.

MIX
Paper | Supporting responsible forestry
FSC™ C104740

This book is dedicated to my mother, Patricia, who had me as a teenager and gave everything so I could be successful. Thank you for reading to me as a child, enriching me with experiences and explicitly teaching me new vocabulary. This book is for you!

About the author

Shareen Wilkinson is executive director of education and leads on curriculum, teaching, and learning and assessment across a multi-academy trust, based in London and Surrey. She has a proven and extensive track record of raising standards in primary schools, particularly for writing, and has worked with schools and local authorities (LAs) across the country. Shareen has been in primary education for over 20 years. In that time, she has fulfilled a wide range of senior leadership roles, including being an LA lead primary adviser and an English adviser. Her subject specialisms are English, assessment, teaching and learning, multi-school leadership and curriculum. She is a fellow of the Chartered College of Teaching and part of the Confederation of Schools Trust (CST) Policy Advisory Group.

Shareen is an established educational author, writer and editor and has written educational resources and books for several leading publishers. Her books focus on English reading, phonics, writing, handwriting and spelling. She has also co-written, with her husband, several story and non-fiction books for pupils in their earliest stages of reading.

For over a decade, Shareen has worked with the Department for Education in various advisory/reviewer roles, including reviewing the DfE writing framework, and as an STA deputy standardisation team leader for the KS2 national writing training.

She is also a KS2 writing moderation manager for a London LA and a KS2 writing moderator.

Please do reach out!
LinkedIn: www.linkedin.com/in/shareen-wilkinson
X/Twitter: @ShareenAdvice
Bluesky: @mrswilkinson.bsky.social

Reviews

Disciplinary Literacy in Primary Schools is a brilliant distillation of an important topic for teachers and leaders. Disciplinary literacy is not always well understood, so this is a timely and valuable book that will prove a boon for busy teachers seeking to develop the literacy knowledge and skills of their pupils. It skilfully synthesises a range of vital literacy topics - from reading, writing, to vocabulary and disciplinary talk - including research, practical tips, and helpful case studies. If you want your pupils to flourish with writing in history, reading in science, or talking in mathematics, then this is the book for you.

Alex Quigley, author and Head of Content & Engagement for the Education Endowment Foundation

This is quite simply excellent. Wilkinson has studied the use of spoken and written language across the curriculum in a powerful and deep study of disciplinary literacy. I highly recommend this to teachers everywhere regardless of phase.

Dame Alison Peacock, Chief Executive, Chartered College of Teaching

This is an extraordinarily important and important book for the primary sector. Underpinned by extensive research, it's also full of beautiful examples of how to help all our pupils to engage with the deep subject matter of a rich curriculum. If leaders and teachers in primary schools use this, engagement, enjoyment and outcomes will increase on all measures.

Mary Myatt, education writer and speaker

What I found incredibly powerful about this brilliant book was how Shareen translates theory into practice providing ways for colleagues, both primary and secondary, to apply the key ideas shared immediately. The chapters on Disciplinary Literacy and Equity, Diversity and Standard English as well as the subject specific examples were so enlightening and exceptional! I recommend this book to everyone interested in enhancing disciplinary literacy practice in schools.

Yamina Bibi, author and former senior leader

Shareen Wilkinson offers a deeply practical and insightful guide for embedding spoken and written language across the curriculum. Her work empowers school leaders with clear strategies to help pupils access, understand and express complex ideas in every subject. A valuable resource for any school committed to equity and excellence.

Fahri Francis, Headteacher, Franciscan Primary School

An invaluable book for any school wishing to embed Disciplinary Literacy. The book explores the key theories behind disciplinary literacy, whilst also providing practical guidance as to what this can look like in the classroom.

James Taylor, Deputy Headteacher, High View Primary School

The primary sector has waited a long time for a 'disciplinary literacy book' that embeds both traditional evidence and finger-on-the-pulse research alongside a wealth of authentic case studies. Wilkinson has managed to draw all of these key ingredients together with a huge helping of common sense. Primary leaders and teachers will welcome a book that values everything that is prioritised in primary schools in such a succinct yet inspiring way. Every subject leader in primary will reach for Wilkinson's work to ensure that children thrive across the curriculum.

Maddy Barnes, Executive Director of English for The Three Saints Trust and English advisor

Wilkinson skilfully examines disciplinary literacy within the primary sector, emphasising the importance of developing schema through high-quality thinking, discussion, reading, and writing across various subject disciplines. The book includes practical implementation ideas, case studies, and an exploration of curriculum design aimed at removing barriers and promoting educational equity for all students. This is an essential read for school leaders.

Áine Donegan, Deputy Headteacher, Allfarthing Primary School

Acknowledgements

Thanks to my husband, Marcus, for always being incredibly supportive and my son Joshua for trialling all the EYFS stories and non-fiction books – we loved the science books.

Thank you to all the case study teachers and senior leaders who gave up their time to share their experiences: Alex Fairlamb, Fahri Francis, Hydeh Fayaz, Juli Ryzop, Louise Pennington, Maria Garcia and Sonia Thompson.

All my colleagues at LEO Academy Trust, who embraced disciplinary literacy in practice, including Phillip Hedger, Amy Carlile, Sophie Gunner, Thomas Strange, Julaan Govier, Rose Maclean, Prathayini Wright, Sam Hughes, Sara Brice, Rachel Teixeira, Rebecca Middleton, Christopher Perrott, Chloe Evans, Giorgia Dibenedetto, Craig Hudson and Emma Potter.

Thank you to the subject associations and organisations, including the Historical Association, Geographical Association, RE Today and Primary STEM Educational Consultancy for your excellent training.

Thank you to Greenshaw Learning Trust for allowing me to attend the secondary disciplinary literacy training and the primary disciplinary literacy training led by Professor Shanahan.

I am very grateful to the team at Hachette Learning for their support and guidance throughout the process, including Tammy Poggo, Anthony Green, Eleanor Weston, Alex Sharratt and Emily Bell.

Contents

About this book xii
A note from the author xiii

Chapter 1: An Introduction to Disciplinary Literacy 1
What could disciplinary literacy look like in primary schools? 3
The importance of building schema from the early years 9
Key tips for implementing disciplinary literacy 12
Disciplinary literacy: knowledge and critical thinking skills 14
Disciplinary literacy and connections with metacognition 17

Chapter 2: Disciplinary Literacy: Equity, Diversity and Standard English 27
Thoughts for consideration 27
Case study example: promoting inclusive and equitable disciplinary literacy with Fahri Francis 32

Chapter 3: Subject-specific Talk or 'Disciplinary Talk' 39
How can we compartmentalise our focus on disciplinary literacy? 44
English speaking and listening 45
Accountable talk 50
Use of technology in communication 52
Disciplinary talk 53

	Case study example: oracy and disciplinary literacy at Key Stage 1: Cheam Park Farm Primary Academy (part of LEO Academy Trust) with Giorgia Dibenedetto 57
Chapter 4:	English 63
	Reading comprehension strategies 64
	Disciplinary reading 68
	Stories across the curriculum 76
	Case study example: implementing disciplinary reading, an interview with Sonia Thompson and Hydeh Fayez 78
	Teaching writing and disciplinary writing 84
	Recommendations 90
	Vocabulary – explicit and implicit approaches 91
Chapter 5:	History 95
	Speaking and thinking like an historian – language frames 97
	Read like an historian 101
	Talk like a historian 104
	Write like an historian 105
	Case study example: disciplinary literacy in history, an interview with Alex Fairlamb 111
Chapter 6:	Science 119
	Speaking and thinking like a scientist – language frames for scientific experiments 120
	Read like a scientist 121
	Science talk time 124
	Write like a scientist 125

Chapter 7: Geography 129
Speaking and thinking like a geographer – language frames 130
Read like a geographer 131
Write like a geographer 132

Chapter 8: *Case study example:* Knowledge Schools Trust, disciplinary literacy – science, history and geography, an interview with Juli Ryzop 137

Chapter 9: Disciplinary Literacy Across the Curriculum 149
Disciplinary literacy in mathematics 149
Disciplinary literacy in religious education (RE) 157

Chapter 10: *Case study example:* implementing disciplinary literacy across an academy trust with Shareen Wilkinson 163
Tips for implementation 173

Appendix: Disciplinary literacy in other subjects 175
Curriculum research bibliography 183
Acronyms and abbreviations 186

About this book

Drawing on the research evidence, *Disciplinary Literacy in Primary Schools* offers both theoretical and practical examples (through case studies and interviews) of how to support primary pupils in reading, writing and speaking across the subject disciplines. Importantly, it incorporates how this might relate to the curriculum in the early years. This book outlines the ways in which teachers can support pupils to read, write and speak like scientists, geographers and historians. It briefly explores other areas across the curriculum. This professional development resource is essential for all Trust leads, senior leaders, local authority advisers, teachers, curriculum leads and English leads who are passionate about having exemplary and equitable practice across the curriculum.

A note from the author

There is no set way of delivering disciplinary literacy in primary schools. It all depends on the quality of English reading and writing teaching and whether the school has an ethos of high expectations for all pupils. Therefore, this book offers a way of teaching disciplinary literacy that has been tried and tested, with example case studies. Schools will need to adapt the strategies to suit the needs of their pupils. Although teachers can dip into the various subjects, it is recommended that the introduction, English and history section is also read to maximise the understanding of disciplinary literacy.

This book is written from a primary practitioner lens, sharing research that I have found over the years. Or research that is currently being advocated centrally. For example, from Ofsted (UK school inspection organisation) or the Department for Education (DfE) guidance. I have shared ideas and strategies that have made implementing disciplinary literacy successful. However, these are tailored to the culture and ethos of schools and groups of schools, so organisations will need to adapt the strategies to their own contexts to ensure that disciplinary literacy is age and stage appropriate.

Chapter 1:
An introduction to disciplinary literacy

Each field of study has its own special ways of using text to create, communicate, and evaluate knowledge…it is vital that students become acquainted with these unique or specialised ways of reading and writing.

(Shanahan, 2019)

Disciplinary literacy explores the ways in which each subject discipline thinks, speaks, writes and reads. The application of this varies across schools, but this book attempts to show a possible approach to this in primary schools. The term disciplinary literacy was originally coined by the Institute of Learning at the University of Pittsburgh in 2002 (McConachie et al, 2010). There are earlier mentions of subject specific skills, but not necessarily using this term, for example, Gee (2004) and Bullock (1975). I am deeply passionate about disciplinary literacy because I have seen how it enables exemplary practice across the curriculum. The principal areas where pupils can complete extended writing within the disciplines are English, history, geography, science and sometimes religious education. Other subjects focus primarily on reading, speaking and thinking within the discipline. There is a difference between reading and writing in English to the complex and often complicated ways that scientists read and write. For example, in English reading, pupils should: make connections; draw inferences; draw on background knowledge; ask questions, visualise; and clarify the meaning of unknown words, as well as monitor comprehension (Bilton et al, 2021, Willingham, 2017, Oakhill et al, 2014, Quigley, 2020 and Tennent, 2014). However, scientists will utilise these strategies, but will also focus on, 'synthesising information, gaining new ideas, evaluating claims, seeking explanations, and deepening understanding ' (Fang and Colosimo, 2024) and historians make interpretations from historical sources or 'compare and contrast' information.

Gabriel and Wenz (2017, p. 3) illuminate disciplinary literacy further:

...rather than developing a general toolbox of literacy skills to apply across disciplines, the goal of disciplinary literacy instruction from this perspective is for adolescents to develop multiple sets of highly specialised literacy tools that allow them to 'read like an historian' or 'write like a scientist'.

Gabriel and Wenz (2017) make an important note that disciplinary literacy is not just about generic literacy skills across the curriculum but about improving and enhancing literacy within other subjects. Pupils are drawing on their knowledge of English reading (e.g. decoding words, reading from left to right) in science, but they are also beginning to learn the way that scientists read. Often, the phrases, 'Speak like a scientist/ historian/artist' etc. are used to describe what this might mean in practice through exploring how scientists or historians carry out their work (Fang & Colosimo, 2024, Shanahan, 2019, Mortimore, 2020). For me, disciplinary literacy is about an ethic of excellence in the primary classroom and accepting high quality work from pupils (Thompson, 2022). From my experience, English and mathematics books tend to be of higher quality than the foundation subjects (e.g. geography, history, religious education, etc.) Disciplinary literacy ensures that pupils are producing exemplary writing/work (and/or oral discussions) in these subjects.

Disciplinary literacy is based on the premise that pupils need both knowledge of facts and timelines (substantive) and knowledge of how historians acquire their knowledge (disciplinary) or subject-specific skills. This distinction of knowledge might not be essential for all subjects, but is an excellent starting point for understanding what historians or scientists might explore at a primary level. Importantly, pupils need to have a strong grasp of English as a subject discipline before embarking on reading and writing across the curriculum, especially in primary schools.

Examples of substantive and disciplinary knowledge:

Substantive knowledge	Disciplinary knowledge
Science knowledge of: – parts of the flower – process of solids, liquids and gases – theory of evolution.	Understanding the skills that scientists need to acquire this knowledge: – predictions – conclusions – analysis – identifying and classifying – making observations – recording data – tables and diagrams.

Other ways of describing knowledge:

- Knowing that – declarative knowledge, e.g. knowing number bonds to 10 or fractions, decimals and percentages (mathematics).
- Knowing how – procedural knowledge, e.g. knowing how to design a webpage (digital skills) (Ofsted, 2021).

The research into disciplinary literacy for primary school pupils as opposed to secondary school research (Ortlieb, E. Kane, B.D. Cheek, E.H. Jr. eds., 2024) is not as extensive, so it requires more guidance for primary teachers. It is the reason why I chose to write this book, in the hope that some of the research can be translated into practice. We are not expecting pupils to be experts at reading or writing like scientists, but we are preparing them for the background knowledge needed to be competent readers, and formal language structures that they will need when they reach secondary school.

What could disciplinary literacy look like in primary schools?

Research on disciplinary literacy for elementary or primary pupils primarily focuses on laying the groundwork for the more advanced subject-specific literacy skills that will be developed in secondary education. Primary teachers might be doing many aspects of 'disciplinary literacy' already but will use different language. I have certainly seen pupils writing across the curriculum, but do not necessarily use this term. Below is a summary of the key discourse from the research.

Building foundational knowledge

The focus for primary pupils is on developing strong foundational literacy skills. Professor Timothy Shanahan and colleagues (2008 and 2014) emphasise that disciplinary literacy depends on basic literacy and advocate a three-tier system, so that it is developmentally appropriate. The information below includes some of the key discourse in this area.

Tier 1 – Basic literacy includes:
- Phonemic awareness
- phonics
- oral reading fluency
- vocabulary and encounters with subject specific vocabulary
- reading comprehension
- early exposure to disciplinary texts, such a stories to introduce concepts.

I would also like to add early mathematical skills.

Tier 2 – Intermediate literacy includes:
- Using increasingly complex spelling strategies (e.g. prefixes and suffixes).
- General reading comprehension strategies (e.g. prediction, summarising and visualising).

Tier 3 – Disciplinary literacy includes:
- Middle and high school pupils learning to read and write within the disciplines.
- Subject-specific literacy and being aware of the different ways that scientists, mathematicians and historians navigate their subject.
- Building 'habits in the mind', enabling pupils to think and speak within a discipline.

(Shanahan et al, 2008 and 2014, Condie et al, 2016, DfES, 2023 and Colwell et al, 2023)

Colwell et al (2023) further break down this approach for elementary or primary pupils into 'core disciplinary skills'. These might be helpful for primary teachers who are wanting to use aspects of disciplinary literacy in their classrooms. In their research paper, they studied the impact of disciplinary literacy on elementary pupils. It concluded that disciplinary literacy was beneficial for pupils, but teachers needed further training to support them with their subject knowledge. The research focused on the following elements of teaching:

- **Recognising and comprehending multiple text types** – understanding the difference between disciplinary texts. Knowing their features so that they support comprehension.
- **Analysing texts** – knowing the different ways that texts can be analysed, e.g. read like a scientist or geographer.
- **Using discipline-specific language** – understanding vocabulary and language structures of the different subject disciplines.
- **Communicating an argument, rationalisation or understanding** – communication of disciplinary knowledge using the style of a particular discipline.

(Source: Colwell et al, 2023)

In summary, while full disciplinary literacy is not a major focus in primary schools, researchers suggest exposing pupils to a variety of disciplinary texts early and having opportunities to analyse texts as well as communicate within the disciplines. The importance of reading historical, scientific or geographical texts has been widely documented as an essential aspect of building background knowledge and thus improving reading comprehension and supporting all pupils to flourish (Willingham, 2017, Oakhill, Cain and Elbro, 2014 and Tennent, 2014). It is not ignoring the fact that pupils need to learn more generalised ways of reading, writing and speaking before they can learn and apply more specialised ways in other subject disciplines. Conversely, research also shows that writing about texts in science, history and literature also enhances both reading comprehension and content learning (Graham and Herbert, 2010).

In a study led by Burke and Kennedy (2024) in Irish primary classrooms, many teachers reported that pupils found the focus on thinking like a scientist or writing like an historian interesting and engaging. Indeed, it offers the opportunity for those who favour history or geography to write about topics that interest them. In the primary years, it is vital that English is mastered, but it is also about building strong literacy connections across the curriculum and enhancing literacy learning (Burke and Kennedy, 2024).

In short, we might not be expecting very young pupils to read and write like we do at KS2, but we can ask disciplinary questions (e.g. *In history, when looking at toys, how is this similar or different to your toys?*) and prepare pupils for the knowledge and vocabulary that they will need in the future, while still embracing the EYFS curriculum. The key aim of the EYFS and KS1 curriculum is to ensure that pupils are competent in their foundational knowledge first. They need to ensure that they can say and write a sentence and are competent at handwriting and spelling (Ofsted, 2024).

Foundational knowledge:
- How to compose simple sentences orally.
- How to hold a pencil correctly and form letters and numbers.
- How to spell.
- How to become a fluent reader.

(Source: Ofsted, 2024)

However, Ippolito et al (2024) in their book *Disciplinary Literacy Inquiry & Instruction*, argue that 'in an age where we are teaching strong foundational skills, we cannot be seduced into believing that phonics and decoding skills alone will translate seamlessly into later sophisticated comprehension and disciplinary literacy skills.' In essence, and this may sound obvious, teaching the foundational knowledge alone may not be enough to secure more complex reading strategies that pupils will need in the later primary years. Pupils need exposure to disciplinary texts from an early age to build the foundations for learning across the disciplines, as mentioned by Shanahan (2008) above.

This includes:
- Providing access or reading aloud non-fiction texts focused on science, history, mathematics, geography and so on.
- Including informational texts in classroom libraries and read-aloud activities.
- Exposing pupils to read various text types and writing for different purposes and audiences.
- Introduction of disciplinary concepts from the early years (covered later in this chapter).

Disciplinary literacy tree (Quigley et al, 2021a and Butlin, 2023)

The Education Endowment Foundation (Quigley et al, 2021a) uses the 'disciplinary literacy tree' to explain the development of these skills, as pupils move through a primary school. This might be helpful for schools when planning disciplinary literacy.

- Early years and KS1: forming the roots with foundational reading and writing skills.
- KS2: the tree begins to branch into different subject domains.

Chapter 1: An introduction to disciplinary literacy

If disciplinary literacy is seen as a fundamental way of improving literacy in secondary classrooms (Quigley et al. 2021a and Moje, 2008) then we can prepare pupils and build on this notion in primary schools. The Education Endowment Foundation (EEF) secondary literacy guidance embodies the notion that 'literacy skills are both general and subject specific' and that all teachers are responsible for teaching reading, writing and speaking within their subject disciplines. This is different in primary, where teachers largely teach all subjects. For this book, the ideas put forward are firmly grounded in primary practice and use the subject-specific aspects of a particular subject according to a school's primary curriculum and the expectations within it. This book does not attempt to teach secondary aspects in primary but embraces the age and stage of the pupils. As Shanahan (2019) explains in his paper on disciplinary literacy in primary schools, complex concepts should be introduced as 'oral language' concepts from the time pupils start school.

The table below exemplifies the subject-specific ways that we might write in primary schools. Indeed, these are pitched to primary level and are the building blocks for the future. This is not an exhaustive list but seeks to exemplify the possible differences.

Write like a writer	Write like a scientist	Write like a geographer	Write like an historian
Content might include: **Fiction** – descriptive vocabulary – metaphors – similes – idioms – adjectives – noun phrases. **Non-fiction** – headings and subheadings – diagrams – expanded noun phrases – formal language. It might also include knowledge of: – audience and purpose – poetry – fiction – non-fiction and draw on research.	Content might include: – scientific vocabulary – predictions – conclusions – analysis – identifying and classifying – making observations – recording data – tables and diagrams. It might also include knowledge of: – plants – the solar system – living things and their habitats – the human digestive system, etc.	Content might include: – geographical vocabulary – collecting, analysing and communicating a range of data – fieldwork – interpreting sources of geographical information – using maps, diagrams, globes and aerial photographs – communicating geographical information through writing at length. It might also include knowledge of: – world countries – rivers, mountains or volcanoes – the water cycle.	Content might include: – historical vocabulary – the concept of continuity and change – making connections, drawing contrasts and analysing trends – structured accounts of events – analysis of events – exploring contrasting arguments and interpretations. It might also include knowledge of: – the Romans – the ancient Greeks – the Victorians, etc.

Generic writing aspects (across all writing)
- Capital letters, full stops and other punctuation.
- Subordinate clauses and multi-clause sentences.
- Heading and sub-headings.
- Paragraphs.
- Formal or academic language.

(Source: Adapted from the Primary National Curriculum for England, 2014)

Further examples of the differences between reading, writing and thinking across the subjects

Lent, R. (2017) Disciplinary literacy: a shift that makes sense. https://ascd.org/el/articles/disciplinary-literacy-a-shift-that-makes-sense (Accessed: 01/04/2025)

Burke, P. and Kennedy, E. (2024) *"Why Do You Think That?" Exploring disciplinary literacy in elementary science, history and visual arts*, Read Teach, 77, 642–652. https://doi.org/10.1002/trtr.2283 (Accessed: 01/04/2025)

The importance of building schema from the early years

If we are to start the concept of disciplinary literacy early in primary schools, then the notion of schema or building a mental model is important. Schema can be described as a mental structure of organising complex bodies of knowledge in the mind. Very often, this concept is not always understood by all teachers, and can lead to a fragmented, rather than sequenced approach to learning throughout the primary years. The Early Years Foundation Stage (EYFS) is the building block and starting point for this learning. These might be basic to begin with, but are deliberately sequenced to build knowledge as pupils move through the primary years. The difference between novices and experts (Haley and Lohr, 2018) is that experts build on the knowledge they already have and connect them together. Novices need concepts to be built up and this needs to be made explicit to them (Benner, 1982). Pupils need to learn new ideas by building on what they already know (Ausubel, 1968).

Cottingham explores how early encounters are important for building schema:

An efficient way to form these complex bodies of knowledge is maybe to teach more generalised ideas first and then help students to connect the details to these ideas.

(Cottinghatt, 2023)

In addition, Ippolito et al (2024) stress the importance of starting early:

We believe that disciplinary literacy ways of thinking and working should be taught in age-appropriate ways as early as kindergarten...these are to adopt habits that can be later refined and shaped.

Importantly, 'once this knowledge has been forged, it acts as an arm which reaches out as a hook to welcome new knowledge.' (Fayez, 2021). Fayez elucidates the fundamental aspect of why starting early is important – it means that pupils can access the curriculum, especially those with special educational needs and those who have not had the opportunity to read widely.

Within nursery and reception classes, pupils are not taught the subjects discretely (for example, history, geography or science). These are covered as part of the Areas of Learning, where knowledge and understanding of the world might be the best connection to these subjects. However, 'it makes sense to consider how early learning in understanding the world will give pupils the foundational concepts and vocabulary to help them to learn geography when they are older.' (Grenier et al, 2023). Early years teachers need to be cognisant of how this might benefit pupils in the future. Additionally, KS1 teachers need to build on those experiences and help pupils to make the connections. For example, a timetable with visual images of what is happening throughout the day in the Reception classroom, might begin the foundations of what chronology means in history. When pupils reach Year 1, teachers can remind pupils that they explored the times of the day in Reception and make these connections for pupils (Grenier et al, 2023).

Although areas such as history, geography and science can be covered by the EYFS Knowledge and Understanding of the World, other areas of learning also support pupils with their background knowledge. Stories have a vital role in promoting communication and language development, but they can also begin to develop a pupil's understanding of the past through exploring fairy tales and taking pupils to different worlds that embed a sense of space and place in geography. Even areas like mathematics can embed the concept of sequencing, which might support the concept of chronology early on. These areas give pupils important experiences and help to build rich schemata as they move through the primary years.

Chapter 1: An introduction to disciplinary literacy

History (monarchy and power)	
Nursery	**Reception**
Literacy – Engage in extended conversations about stories, learning new vocabulary (historical stories, fairy tales, and stories that build rich schemata) **Mathematics** – Begin to describe a sequence of events, real or fictional, using words such as 'first', 'then…' (concept of chronology) **Knowledge and understanding of the world** Begin to make sense of their own life-story and family's history – Show interest in different occupations (e.g. superheroes link to significant people in history) – Make connections between the features of their family and other families	**Physical development** – Dressing up as kings and queens **Literacy** – Know that in fairy tales kings/queens are important, powerful people who rule over others **Year 1 and/or 2** – To know that a monarch in the UK is a king or queen – To begin to understand that power is exercised in different ways in different cultures, times and groups, e.g. monarchy – To know that Britain was organised into kingdoms and these were governed by monarchs
Blandishment	
Pupils have no schemata to draw on	

In the first example, the substantive concepts of monarchy and power can be explored with young pupils in most areas of learning. This might start with reading stories about kings and queens, dressing up in the role-play area and drawing on pupils' own family stories to build a sense of hierarchy. This puts pupils in a stronger position to learn about monarchy and power as they move through the primary years, and certainly prepares them in Years 1 and 2 where they might study kings and queens in more depth. There is a case for exploring concepts. For example, 'adult interaction is crucial. We need to think about how we help pupils to develop their early scientific skills in observation.' (Grenier et al, 2023). These earlier encounters support pupils to build on their new knowledge. If they have no schema to draw on, like a novice learner being presented with the word 'blandishment' (intentionally flattering or pleasing action) without reference to prior knowledge, then it might take pupils longer to embed knowledge into their long-term memory. Yet, if we make connections to real life experiences, then 'blandishment' might not be so abstract at all and seeks to expand a pupil's vocabulary.

Among this knowledge are what we call 'substantive concepts'. These are concepts that that can be explored across any historical event. For example, if we look at the concept of 'power', this can be explored from Nursery to KS2 and beyond and across different historical events.

Substantive concept: power and monarchy:

Nursery	Reception	Year 1	Year 2
Dressing up as kings and queens Reading fairy tales	Reading fairy tales Exploring their own families Superheroes (links to significant people)	Exploring Queen Elizabeth II	Exploring Henry VIII

There do not seem to be any agreements about what substantive concepts to study. However, the ones that are frequently explored are power, migration, hierarchy, beliefs and trade.

Key tips for implementing disciplinary literacy

Before embarking on implementing disciplinary literacy across the primary curriculum and gaining the benefits (see appendix), there some key fundamentals that need to be in place, for it to be successfully fulfilled. Here are my suggestions:

- In primary schools, where we typically teach most subjects and have the same teachers, there might be some overlap with other subjects and some cross-curricular writing. It really does not matter and we should not be pedantic, especially in KS1! The aim is to prepare pupils and for them to gain a deeper understanding of the subject disciplines.
- Disciplinary literacy relies on an excellent English curriculum. Schools need to ensure that they are teaching high quality English lessons, where pupils are taught to read, write and speak to a high standard. This will make it easier to seamlessly move to other subjects. Of course, adaptations should be made to the curriculum so that all pupils can achieve.
- Teachers and pupils need to work out what the substantive and disciplinary knowledge is for each subject. It might not be necessary for subjects like English or music.
- There is no expectation that EYFS and KS1 pupils will write long and detailed essays. Disciplinary literacy needs to be age and stage

appropriate. It might start off as oral at first, with short sentences that are within a particular discipline.
- Beyond disciplinary literacy, an excellent curriculum should be sequenced and progressive and build rich schemata. For example, learning about how plants grow in nursery will support pupils when they explore the parts of plants in more depth when they reach KS1. Teachers and schools have deliberately considered how learning can be built upon.
- From experience, explicit and implicit teaching of vocabulary needs to be embedded and discussed across the curriculum. A key part of disciplinary literacy is to use, apply and understand key vocabulary to access core concepts. For example, learning about the terms 'evaporation' and 'condensation' in science is important for building knowledge.
- For other subjects, the work produced should be within the discipline, even if pupils are not writing at any length.
- Taking part in disciplinary literacy should not prevent a topic or thematic approach to the curriculum. Schools can still link subjects and topics where they are relevant. Similarly, disciplinary literacy can still continue as part of continuous provision in KS1.

As pupils progress through primary school, and from looking at the research, I feel there is an opportunity for primary teachers and leaders to:

- Explore subject-specific vocabulary.
- Ask and answer disciplinary questions.
- Deliberately sequence the curriculum so that it is progressive and builds on what pupils already know.
- Read non-fiction texts to pupils and use texts to explore disciplinary concepts, e.g. read a book about the life cycle in science.
- Analyse and discuss the key features of disciplinary texts.
- Begin to write within the discipline, especially by the end of KS2.
- Discover how different disciplines approach debates and arguments.

All these aspects are covered throughout the book as part of the main text or are within the case studies and interviews.

Further information on primary school disciplinary literacy

Bedrock Learning (2022): Disciplinary literacy tips from primary and secondary experts. https://primary.bedrocklearning.org/literacy-blogs/disciplinary-literacy-tips-from-literacy-experts/ (Accessed: 04/04/25)

Collier, K. (2023) Empowering elementary students with disciplinary literacy. www.edutopia.org/article/disciplinary-literacy-empowers-elementary-students (Accessed: 04/04/25)

Wilkinson, S. (2025) Disciplinary literacy – how senior leaders can implement it. www.teachwire.net/news/disciplinary-literacy-how-to-primary/ (Accessed: 10/5/25)

Disciplinary literacy: knowledge and critical thinking skills

The disciplinary literacy approach sits firmly within the notion of understanding the subject disciplines as part of a knowledge-rich curriculum as opposed to a set of generalised skills. Knowledge-rich can be simplified as a 'well-sequenced curriculum that is underpinned by an understanding of how children learn… it must be based on a rich conception of knowledge that includes the skills and attitudes that contribute to success.' (Quigley, 2019). It emphasises the importance of careful sequencing and coherence, explicit teaching and long-term retention of knowledge. In addition, it facilitates critical thinking skills. This section will touch on the discourse on having a core knowledge curriculum and explore some of the critiques around this curriculum approach.

Back in 2013, when the notion of a core knowledge curriculum was first introduced centrally to schools, the work of E.D. Hirsch was frequently referenced. Hirsch, who is the founder of the Core Knowledge Foundation, has been an influence upon the current curriculum focus in England (Hirsch, 2003). Hirsch's theory is that subject-specific knowledge (or domain knowledge) is a foundation for new knowledge, helping students commit this knowledge to long-term memory, and that core knowledge emphasises specific information that pupils need to learn, e.g. important events in history. The quote below exemplifies his theory on domain knowledge:

If we are reading a story about a baseball game in the newspaper sports section, we must typically know quite a lot about baseball to comprehend what is being said. Words have multiple purposes and their meaning in a particular instance is cued by the reader's domain knowledge.

(Hirsch, 2003, p.17)

Hirsch (2003) intimates that the language used by baseball players will be more comprehensive for pupils who have the domain knowledge of how to play baseball than those who are not exposed. He also describes comprehension strategies, such as inference and deduction, predicting or classifying, as insignificant after time (Hirsch, 2003). By devoting a small amount of time to comprehension strategies and focussing on domain knowledge, Hirsch (2003) states that this will be sufficient in improving reading comprehension, especially for pupils from poorer backgrounds.

However, a knowledge-rich curriculum also needs to be aware of diversity. Kara (2024) in her book, *The Diverse Curriculum*, calls for educators to be conscious of what the purported 'core' knowledge entails. Schema development (discussed earlier in this chapter) can be positive, but it can also form negative stereotypes of groups in society. How do young pupils develop schemata about disability or race? Does the curriculum represent groups who have been erased from the core knowledge of the national curriculum. For example, what scientists are represented and are seen as important? Although the focus on core knowledge is well meaning, it does need to address and notice issues of diversity and inclusion that make all pupils feel like they belong in the curriculum. Perhaps Christine Counsell's (2018) notion of 'core' and 'hinterland' knowledge is useful here. Essentially, the core is the key knowledge that pupils need to know, the stuff that they will remember. The hinterland is the background, which could be a 'story' that benefits the core. Earlier in this chapter, we looked at the importance of building schema in the early years and these earlier experiences of reading stories, etc. help to build the hinterland knowledge. Thus, educators need to be clear about what 'core' and 'hinterland' knowledge pupils are learning and how this embraces diversity and respects others. This notion is explored further in the section on equity and inclusion.

Another key critique refers explicitly to what Claxton (2007) might term, 'building young people's capacity to learn' or 'learning to learn'. This includes the kinds of attributes and dispositions needed for all subjects, for example, 'resilience; resourcefulness; reflectiveness and reciprocity' (Claxton, 2004). This also entails critical thinking, problem solving and collaborative working. Claxton (2024) emphasises the importance of both aspects of knowledge, 'the conclusion from work in cognitive science is straightforward: we must ensure that pupils acquire background knowledge in parallel with practising critical thinking skills.' Furthermore, Alexander (2010) comments that, 'pupils do not need to know lots of dates. They can look that information up on Google and store it on their mobile phones.' Skills are depicted as a way for pupils to develop their creative and critical thinking, so that they are independent thinkers, supporting future flexibility (Alexander, 2010 and Vail, 1997).

Hargreaves (2001) comments that young people will need lifelong learning skills to meet the demands of a changing working environment, 'teachers and schools must stop serving as role models of fading career structures…and begin to model people who are team-playing, networking and community-supporting.' Moreover, Lawton (1998) comments that there is an important gap between knowledge and twenty-first century skills needed for the changing environment in which we live. In addition, Trilling and Fadel (2009) strongly recommend that young people and pupils need learning skills, information and technology skills and life or career skills. There are many academics who are interested in developing transferable skills needed for work and future roles.

Another perspective is seen by Fang and Colosimo (2024). They argue that disciplinary literacy will prepare pupils for being citizens of the world and for current scientific issues that appear in the media: 'headlines in newspapers and websites require critical analysis as these reports can be distorted from the original source.' Being able to analyse sources and have a critical view of what is happening will be a key skill within the digital age, where information is freely available. Brock et al (2014) explain that young pupils are accessing content online and that we need to support pupils to take a 'critical stance' when encountering texts online and in print. This means that the need for critical analysis and checking sources of evidence is even more pertinent for the digital age.

Although the discourse presents a dichotomy between knowledge and skills, Yandell (2023) dispels this myth by stating the following:

- Knowledge and skills are interdependent, not opposing forces.
- Critical thinking and problem-solving require a strong knowledge base.

As an educator, there is space for both to co-exist if we are to truly empower our young pupils. This is especially true in the early years where so much is focused on self-regulation and building independence skills. For example, putting on your coat and washing your hands. Early years pupils need a focus on life-skills to thrive in the future. In primary, our curriculum enrichment opportunities (e.g. attending trips, forest school and sporting events), as well as a sequenced and progressive curriculum, enable pupils to build resilience and critical thinking skills.

Further reading

Counsell, C. (2018). Blog. Senior Curriculum Leadership 1: The indirect manifestation of knowledge: (A) curriculum as narrative. https://thedignityofthethingblog.wordpress.com/2018/04/07/senior-curriculum-leadership-1-the-indirect-manifestation-of-knowledge-a-curriculum-as-narrative/ (Accessed: 04/04/25)

Disciplinary literacy and connections with metacognition

Metacognition is specifically about the ways learners can monitor and purposefully direct their learning, for example by deciding that a particular strategy for memorisation is likely to be successful, monitor whether it has indeed been successful, and then deliberately change (or not change) their memorisation method based on that evidence.

(Muijs, 2020)

As discussed, disciplinary literacy has many benefits, both for subjects and for future learning, and it is also a metacognitive approach. The research into metacognition is extensive and has been recognised as a proven way of supporting pupils with making rapid progress in the classroom, culminating into 8+ months progress for primary pupils (Quigley et al, 2021b). Disciplinary literacy (or subject-specific reading, writing, speaking and thinking) is a form of metacognition where pupils need to plan, evaluate and monitor their work. A detailed knowledge of a subject and being able to articulate your thought-process is a key aspect of metacognition.

METACOGNITION
My knowledge of *myself* (my approach to maths problems); the *task* (what do I know about this type of problem); and *strategies* (different ways to solve them).

1. Planning:
'I need to think about how we have done these problems before and choose the best strategy.
... I know, I'll start by writing the problem as an algebraic equation.'

TASK:
Mason and Jasmine have £5 between them. Mason has 90p more than Jasmine. How much money does Jasmine have?

COGNITION
Translating the words into an equation.

3. Evaluation
'Writing out the equations has successfully moved me on to the next step with this task.'

2. Monitoring
'Has this improved my understanding of the task?
Yes, it now looks like a type of problem I'm familiar with: a simultaneous equation.'

Figure 1.1 Using a maths question to demonstrate metacognition

(Source: Quigley, A., Muijs, D. & Stringer, E. (2021b). from: Metacognition and Self-Regulated Learning: Guidance Report. Education Endowment Foundation)

The example above demonstrates how pupils are encouraged to articulate their thought-process when planning, monitoring and evaluating their strategies. It can be more helpful for pupils to shorten this to, 'plan, do and review'. From the example, it is about articulating your thought-process. Metacognition is time limited and is not needed to be made explicit once pupils have mastered a concept. However, for pupils with special educational needs in mainstream classrooms, the EEF (2021b) guidance states that metacognition, with a particular focus on explicit instruction, is particularly powerful.

How do the seven steps of metacognition fit into the disciplinary literacy?

The seven-step process of metacognition fits in perfectly with any disciplinary literacy in the classroom. To be able to speak like a scientist or historian requires detailed knowledge of the subject discipline which can be enabled through explicit teaching. Several schools use the gradual release of responsibility to model this (for example, 'I do, We do, You do'), which is a cyclical process (Fisher and Frey, 2010), and the seven-steps help to break this down further. Throughout my career, the main area that is missed out, is the 'I do' section where teachers and other adults need to explicitly model their thought-process. This is essential for disciplinary literacy because pupils will need plenty of examples and scaffolds to support them with their own work within the disciplines.

To illustrate this it is helpful to look at the seven-step model for teaching metacognitive strategies (Table 1.1).

Table 1.1 The seven-step model for teaching metacognitive strategies

Strategy: Taken from Quigley et al (2021b)	History: Speaking like an historian	English: Speaking like a reader	Mathematics: Thinking and speaking like a mathematician
Activating prior knowledge	The teacher draws on knowledge of past monarchs when looking at historical significance. *'I recall that significant people impact our lives today.'*	The teacher draws on their predictions for the text when reading. *'I think this is going to be about… because this reminds me of…'*	The teacher draws on knowledge of past word problems. *'I remember using this strategy.'*

Strategy: Taken from Quigley et al (2021b)	History: Speaking like an historian	English: Speaking like a reader	Mathematics: Thinking and speaking like a mathematician
Explicit strategy instruction	The teacher models their thought-process when writing about an historically significant monarch. Modelling the planning and reviewing process. 'I am going to use this word because... I do not want informal language here because...'	The teacher models their thought-process whilst reading a text, using reading comprehension strategies. Modelling questioning and ideas. 'I wonder what this word means?' 'I think that she is lonely in this part of the story because...'	The teacher models their thought-process and articulates the calculations, estimates and strategies they are going to use.
Modelling of learned strategy	The teacher uses the notes and discussion on a significant monarch to write the first section, focusing on *Who? What? Where?* and *Why?*	The teacher continues to model the 'think aloud' strategy. Focussing on important ways to read a text, e.g. visualise, make predictions, summarise etc.	The teacher models the strategy for working out the calculation.
Memorisation of learned strategy	The teacher discusses the first section of writing through purposeful talk time. 'Why is this person significant? What have I used to demonstrate this?'	The teacher encourages talk time though discussing the text.	The teacher encourages talk time through discussing and critiquing the strategy she/he has used or has used an example to critique.
Guided practice	The teacher models the second section with the whole class and asks for ideas to contribute.	The teacher continues to model, encouraging the pupils to contribute to the discussion.	The teacher reviews another calculation and the pupils work as a class to look at the steps to completing it.

Strategy: Taken from Quigley et al (2021b)	History: Speaking like an historian	English: Speaking like a reader	Mathematics: Thinking and speaking like a mathematician
Independent practice	Pupils complete their own disciplinary writing and review whether they have been successful.	Pupils use reading comprehension strategies and review whether they have been successful. They summarise key aspects that they have learned.	Pupils use the problem-solving strategy to complete their own calculations and review whether they have been successful.

Disciplinary literacy is also based on having a progressive and sequenced curriculum, having strong teaching and learning strategies and reading extensively across the curriculum. Opportunities to read about the subject and the use of technology to further enhance learning, e.g. virtual maps or places around the world, further support the success of disciplinary literacy.

References and bibliography

Alexander, R. (ed.) (2010) *Children, Their World, Their Education: Final Report and Recommendations of the Cambridge Primary Review.* Routledge.

Ausubel, D.P. (1968) *Educational Psychology: a Cognitive View.* Holt, Rinehart and Winston.

Benner, P. (1982) 'From novice to expert', *American Journal of Nursing,* 82(3), 402–7.

Bilton, C., & Duff, A. (2021) Improving Literacy in KS2: Guidance Report. Education Endowment Foundation. https://d2tic4wvo1iusb.cloudfront.net/production/eef-guidance-reports/literacy-ks2/EEF-Improving-literacy-in-key-stage-2-report-Second-edition.pdf?v=1712494070 (Accessed: 04/04/25)

Brock, C. H., Goatley, V. J., Raphael, T. E., Trost-Shahata, E., & Weber, C. M. (2014) *Engaging Students in Disciplinary Literacy, K-6: Reading, Writing, and Teaching Tools for the Classroom.* Teachers College Press.

Burke, P. and Kennedy, E. (2024) "Why Do You Think That?" Exploring disciplinary literacy in elementary science, history and visual arts.

Read Teach, 77: 642–652. https://doi.org/10.1002/trtr.2283 (Accessed: 04/04/25)

Butlin, C. (2023). EEF blog. Demystifying disciplinary literacy. A root and branch approach. https://educationendowmentfoundation.org.uk/news/demystifying-disciplinary-literacy-a-root-and-branch-approach (Accessed: 04/04/25)

Claxton, G. (2024) *The Future of Teaching and the Myths That Hold Us Back*. Routledge.

Colwell, J. (2019) Selecting texts for disciplinary literacy instruction. *The Reading Teacher*, 72(5), 631–637. doi:10.1002/trtr.1762 (Accessed: 04/04/25)

Colwell, J., Hutchison, A., & Woodward, L. (2023) Examining a Phased Planning Approach to Support Elementary Preservice Teachers in Disciplinary Literacy-Focused Instruction. *Literacy Research: Theory, Method, and Practice*, 72(1), 161–178. https://journals.sagepub.com/doi/full/10.1177/23813377231183419 (Accessed: 04/04/25)

Condie, C. & Ippolito, J. (2016) Encouraging our youngest students to think like scientists: Exploring elementary teachers' experiences of teaching disciplinary literacy. Massachusetts Reading Association. www.academia.edu/26862708/Encouraging_our_youngest_students_to_think_like_scientists_Exploring_elementary_teachers_experiences_of_teaching_disciplinary_literacy?email_work_card=title (Accessed: 04/04/25)

Cottinghatt, S. (2023) Constructing Schemas. In Jones, K. eds. *The ResearchED Guide to Cognitive Science: An Evidence-informed Guide for Teachers*. Hodder Education.

Counsell, C. (2018). Blog. Senior Curriculum Leadership 1: The indirect manifestation of knowledge: (A) curriculum as narrative. https://thedignityofthethingblog.wordpress.com/2018/04/07/senior-curriculum-leadership-1-the-indirect-manifestation-of-knowledge-a-curriculum-as-narrative/ (Accessed: 04/04/25)

Deng, Z. (2022) Powerful knowledge, educational potential and knowledge-rich curriculum: pushing the boundaries. *Journal of Curriculum Studies*, 54(5), 599–617.

Department for Education, England (2023). The Reading Framework https://assets.publishing.service.gov.uk/media/65830c10ed3c34000d3bfcad/The_reading_framework.pdf (Accessed: 04/04/25)

English Association (2024). The English Association's response to the Commission on the Future of Oracy Education. https://englishassociation.ac.uk/the-english-associations-response-to-the-commission-on-the-future-of-oracy-education/ (Accessed: 04/04/25)

Fang, Z. & Colosimo, N. (2024) Promoting Science Literacy though Reading: A Disciplinary Literacy Approach. In Ortlieb, E., Kane, B.D. & Cheek, E.H. Jr. (2024) *Disciplinary Literacies: Unpacking Research, Theory, and Practice*. Guilford Publications.

Fayez, H. (2021). EEF blog. Working with schemas and why it matters to teachers. https://educationendowmentfoundation.org.uk/news/eef-blog-working-with-schemas-and-why-it-matters-to-teachers (Accessed: 04/04/25)

Fisher, D., & Frey, N. (2010) *Better Learning Through Structured Teaching: A Framework for the Gradual Release of Responsibility*. ASCD.

Gabriel, R. & Wenz, C. (2017) Three directions for disciplinary literacy. *Educational leadership: Journal of the Department of Supervision and Curriculum Development*, N.E.A 74(5) www.researchgate.net/publication/316926851_Three_Directions_for_Disciplinary_Literacy (Accessed: 04/04/25)

Gee, J. P. (2004) *Situated Language and Learning: A Critique of Traditional Schooling*. Routledge.

Goldman, S. R., Britt, M. A., Brown, W., Cribb, G., George, M., Greenleaf, C., Lee, C. D., Shanahan, C., & Project READI (2016). Disciplinary literacies and learning to read for understanding: A conceptual framework of core processes and constructs. *Educational Psychologist*, 51, 219–246.

Grenier, J., O'Sullivan, J., Pemberton, L. & Bradbury, A. (2022) Understanding the World in Grenier, J. & Vollans, C. *Putting the EYFS Curriculum into Practice*. SAGE Publications.

Grenier, J. & Vollans, C. (2022) *Putting the EYFS Curriculum Into Practice*. SAGE Publications.

Haley, Karen J. & Lohr, Kathy D. (2018) Novice and expert: challenging professional education. *The Journal of Continuing Higher Education*, 66:3, 200–203, DOI: 10.1080/07377363.2018.1525520.

Hargreaves, A. & Goodson, I. (2006) 'Educational change over time? The sustainability and non-sustainability of three decades of secondary school change and continuity'. *Education Administration Quarterly*, 42 (3), 3–41.

Graham, S. & Herbert, M. (2010) Writing to read: evidence for how writing can improve reading: a report from Carnegie Corporation of New York. Alliance for Excellent Education. https://acuresearchbank.acu.edu.au/item/8v6x5/writing-to-read-evidence-for-how-writing-can-improve-reading-a-report-from-carnegie-corporation-of-new-york (Accessed: 04/04/25)

Hirsch, E.D. (2003) Reading comprehension requires knowledge of words and the world. *American Federation of Teachers*, 10–44. www.aft.org/sites/default/files/Hirsch.pdf (Accessed: 04/04/25)

Hirsch, E.D. (2004) *The New First Dictionary of Cultural Literacy: What Your Child Needs to Know*. Houghton Mifflin Company.

Ippolito, J., Dobbs, C. L. & Charner-Laird, M. (2024) *Disciplinary Literacy Inquiry & Instruction*, Second Edition. (n.p.): Harvard Education Press.

Jones, K. eds. (2023). *The ResearchED Guide to Cognitive Science: An Evidence-informed Guide for Teachers*. Hodder Education.

McConachie, S. M. & Petrosky, T. (2010) *Content Matters: A Disciplinary Literacy Approach to Improving Student Learning*. Wiley.

Moje (2008) Foregrounding the disciplines in secondary literacy teaching and learning: a call for change. *Journal of Adolescent & Adult Literacy*, 52(2).

Mortimore, K. (2020) *Disciplinary Literacy and Explicit Vocabulary Teaching: A Whole School Approach to Closing the Attainment Gap*. Hodder Education.

Oakhill J, Cain K, Elbro C. (2014) *Understanding and Teaching Reading Comprehension: a Handbook*. Routledge.

Ofsted (2021) Research review series: science. www.gov.uk/government/publications/research-review-series-science/research-review-series-science (Accessed: 04/04/25)

Ofsted (2024) Strong Foundations in the first years of school. www.gov.uk/government/publications/strong-foundations-in-the-first-years-of-school/strong-foundations-in-the-first-years-of-school (Accessed: 04/04/25)

Ortlieb, E., Kane, B.D. & Cheek, E.H. Jr. eds. (2024) *Disciplinary Literacies: Unpacking Research, Theory, and Practice.* Guilford Publications.

Quigley, A. (2019). Blog. What do we mean by knowledge rich anyway? https://educationendowmentfoundation.org.uk/news/eef-blog-what-do-we-mean-by-knowledge-rich-anyway (Accessed: 04/04/25)

Quigley, A. (2020) *Closing the Reading Gap* (1st ed.). Routledge.

Quigley, A.& Coleman, R. (2021a) Improving Literacy in Secondary Schools: Guidance Report. Education Endowment Foundation. https://d2tic4wvo1iusb.cloudfront.net/production/eef-guidance-reports/literacy-ks3-ks4/EEF_KS3_KS4_LITERACY_GUIDANCE.pdf?v=1712491708 (Accessed: 04/04/25)

Quigley, A., Muijs, D. & Stringer, E. (2021b) Metacognition and Self-Regulated Learning: Guidance Report. Education Endowment Foundation. https://d2tic4wvo1iusb.cloudfront.net/production/eef-guidance-reports/metacognition/EEF_Metacognition_and_self-regulated_learning.pdf?v=1724004610 (Accessed: 04/04/25)

Shanahan, T., & Shanahan, C. (2008) Teaching disciplinary literacy to adolescents: Rethinking content-area literacy, *Harvard Educational Review*, 78(1), 40–59.

Shanahan, C., Shanahan, T., & Misichia, C. (2011) Analysis of expert readers in three disciplines: History, mathematics, and chemistry, *Journal of Literacy Research*, 3, 393–429.

Shanahan, C. & Shanahan, T. (2014) Does disciplinary literacy have a place in elementary school? *The Reading Teacher*, 67(8), 636–639.

Shanahan, T. (2019) Disciplinary Literacy in Primary Schools. https://ncca.ie/media/4679/disciplinary-literacy-in-the-primary-school-professor-timothy-shanahan-university-of-illinois-at-chicago-1.pdf (Accessed: 04/04/25)

Tennent, W. (2014) *Understanding Reading Comprehension: Processes and Practices*. SAGE Publications.

Thompson, S. (2022) *Berger's an Ethic of Excellence in Action Series*. John Catt (Hodder).

Trilling, B. & Fadel, C. (2009) *21st Century Skills: Learning for Life in our Times*. Wiley.

Vail, K. (1997) Core comes to Crooksville, *American School Board Journal*, 184(3), pp.14–18.

Willingham, D. T. (2009) *Why don't students like school?* JosseyBass.

Willingham, D. T. (2017) *The Reading Mind: A Cognitive Approach to Understanding How the Mind Reads*. Wiley.

Wolsey, T. D. & Lapp, D. (2024) *Literacy in the Disciplines: A Teacher's Guide for Grades 5–12*. Guilford Publications.

Yandell, J. (2023) English and the Knowledge Question (Revisited). *Changing English*. www.tandfonline.com/doi/epdf/10.1080/1358684X.2022.2164254?needAccess=true (Accessed: 04/04/25)

Chapter 2:
Disciplinary literacy: equity, diversity and Standard English

Asking students to exchange their lifeworld language for the specialist language of the discipline even for a moment is requiring students to give part of themselves and put parts of their identity on hold.

(Williams and Martinez, 2024)

Thoughts for consideration

It is noted that some of the literature around disciplinary literacy needs to be cognisant of all voices, including ethnic minority voices, those where English is an additional language and those from disadvantaged backgrounds. Critiques of disciplinary literacy argue that it is a set standard way of thinking, speaking and reading, 'dismissing cultural and linguistic ways of knowing and showing' (Williams and Martinez, 2024). The implication here is that disciplinary literacy mainly 'upholds the white middle-class' way of communicating as the only way of speaking across the subject disciplines and is steeped in 'historical legacies of colonialism' (Williams and Martinez, 2024). Others have critiqued the wider issue of policing how those from minoritised groups speak, 'Marginalised children routinely experience the hostile policing of their language and public humiliation for their purported inability to speak correctly.' (Cushing, 2024). Gaunt (2025) further explicates this notion of encouraging pupils' confidence and pride in their authentic voices, regardless of linguistic background. All these perspectives are worth considering in the wider aspects of developing disciplinary literacy and to not prescribe to a single narrative. However, it is also worth considering that not everyone speaks the same and pupils from disadvantaged backgrounds and/or minoritised groups can read, write and spell well because they are not one homogenous group. In other words, they do not all have the same beliefs and ways of doing things. In society, pupils do need to navigate the world of work and unfortunately, it does not matter how educated you are. Pupils need to be able to adapt and tweak their register (vocabulary and grammar) using Standard English depending on the situation they in.

The notion of using Standard English in classrooms has had a long history. Basil Bernstein's work on language, control and identity may illuminate why a focus on Standard English may be tied to middle-class values. Bernstein argues that educational success is largely tied to social class (Bernstein, 2000 and 2003). Clark (2010) expresses that Bernstein's theory is shown in England's schools because, 'language is inextricably linked to notions of social class and Standard English is associated with the middle-class values' (Clark, 2010, p. 38). Therefore, a focus on Standard English might be used to uphold social order and impart middle-class ideologies about how we should speak and therefore behave. In relation to how we speak, Halliday (1989) would argue that pupils should be given a 'grammar of choice' (my emphasis) and that they may change their spoken grammar according to the social context they are in. For example, a different dialect may be used when speaking in school to when speaking with peers.

Additionally, McCartney and Carter (2006) have produced a corpus, which is a large collection of primarily spoken texts that explicates the differences between spoken and written grammar. During a conference on grammar I attended, Professor Carter argued that pupils should be taught the differences between spoken and written grammar so that they are able to articulate their writing clearly (Carter, 1998 and Hudson, 1992). By the end of year 6, pupils are taught the difference between spoken and written language, especially within writing, where varying their levels of formality is a focus.

With disciplinary literacy seen as a fundamental way of improving reading and writing for all groups, particularly underachieving groups, it is important for teachers to practise the 'discipline of noticing' (Williams and Martinez, 2024). More specifically, 'noting' for issues of equality and diversity within the work that we do. *How can we promote equity and inclusion at the same time as exploring disciplinary literacy?* This is about avoiding unnecessary stereotypes and respecting viewpoints from different pupils within our classrooms. Being deliberate about representations of scientists, historians and geographers across the curriculum and ensuring that pupils feel a sense of belonging. It means exploring a wider range of British people from diverse backgrounds. For example, when studying science, looking at famous male and female scientists and those from ethnic minority groups. This is not about excluding people like David Attenborough but being aware of people like Mary Anning and Dame Margaret Aderin-Pocock.

An example of this work is when teachers create resources for pupils. It took me two years to work on the *'Speak like a...'* posters at LEO Academy Trust. They were originally designed to support teachers and pupils with their disciplinary knowledge of subjects as pupils were only recalling facts and statistics and needed to understand disciplinary knowledge and vocabulary. A key part of the resource was to create real-life historians, scientists, mathematicians, etc. who were diverse and reflected society. For example, we showed Stephen Hawkins, David Olusoga, Mary Anning and Freida Kahlo. They are established and accomplished, but also represent talent, disability, a diverse heritage and female scientists and artists, etc.

Here are some questions for consideration:

English
- Are the narratives selected wide and varied? Think about whether they only represent trauma, Black exceptionalism, American literature as opposed to British literature or are historical, and how they might be perceived.
- Are female authors represented in the literature that pupils are reading?
- Does the portrayal of certain genders in texts represent known stereotypes?
- Are the diverse texts selected representative of non-fiction, fiction and poetry and not limited to one type of writing, e.g. poetry?
- If you work in a non-diverse school, do you have a diverse range of texts within the English curriculum? This is important because it prepares pupils for the society that they may live in. In addition, this is not about using tokenistic texts. They must be chosen for their quality and enhance pupils' knowledge and understanding of literature.
- Do pupils learn about both formal and informal writing and the difference between speech and writing – especially at KS2?

(Adapted from: Wilkinson, S. 2021).

History
- When studying history, who is represented in your curriculum? Are there a varied and diverse range of historians being represented?
- Are our historians from a range of backgrounds? Do they show people of colour?
- Is Black and Asian British history and history from other underrepresented groups, interwoven into British history, e.g. people of colour who contributed to WWII.
- These questions can also be explored with other subjects.

Science
- Are scientists explored from different British backgrounds so that they are not seen as one homogenous group, e.g. white and male?

General curriculum questions
- In EYFS, do we show dolls that reflect inclusion (e.g. disability or dolls of colour)?
- Does the curriculum give the full picture? E.g. historical origins of numbers in mathematics or designers from different backgrounds.
- Is disability, LGBT+ representation and people from minoritised groups seamlessly woven into the curriculum? Not a bolt on or a special month, but people from these groups who are seamlessly integrated into the people who represent the disciplines.

Further reading and resources

Historical Association. (2019) How diverse is your history curriculum? www.history.org.uk/primary/resource/9620/how-diverse-is-your-history-curriculum (Accessed: 04/04/25)

Holdstock, K. (2024) *Teaching a Diverse Primary Art Curriculum: A Practical Guide to Help Teachers*. Bloomsbury Publishing Plc.

Institute of Physics. Diversity and Inclusion. https://www.iop.org/about/news/iop-diversity-and-inclusion (Accessed: 04/04/25)

Kara, B. (2024) *Diversity in the Curriculum*. Sage Publications.

Louis, S., & Betteridge, H. (2024) *Let's Talk About Race in the Early Years*. Taylor & Francis.

Chapter 2: Disciplinary literacy: equity, diversity and Standard English

Wilkinson, S. (2021). Key take-aways from the Lit in Colour research on diversity in reading. https://educationblog.oup.com/primary/key-take-aways-from-the-lit-incolour-research-on-diversity-in-reading (Accessed: 04/04/25)

Case study example: promoting inclusive and equitable disciplinary literacy with Fahri Francis

Fahri Francis: headteacher, Franciscan Primary School and ITT English tutor

Background

Franciscan Primary School, located in south London, is a vibrant and diverse educational institution serving 285 pupils across Nursery to Year 6. The school community is characterised by a high proportion of pupils from ethnic minority backgrounds, with 91.9% of pupils identifying as not White British and 57.5% speaking a first language other than English. A significant number of pupils (37.9%) are eligible for free school meals, highlighting the socioeconomic diversity within the school. Additionally, 28.8% of pupils receive special educational needs (SEN) support, further reflecting the school's inclusive ethos.

At Franciscan Primary School, they prioritise promoting equality and inclusion within disciplinary literacy. This involves a conscious effort to challenge systemic biases and create an inclusive learning environment that values diverse voices. Their approach is data-driven and informed by research, ensuring their practices are effective and equitable.

Case study example: promoting inclusive and equitable disciplinary literacy

Research and data-driven support

Data from pupil demographics and performance is used to tailor their disciplinary literacy initiatives. By analysing patterns in pupil achievement, attendance and engagement, they identify areas where additional support is needed. This data-driven approach allows them to implement targeted interventions and measure their impact, ensuring that their strategies are effective in addressing the needs of their diverse student body.

Organising disciplinary literacy – what does it look like in practice?

To enable an inclusive and equitable disciplinary literacy environment, they focus on several key areas:

1 Franciscan Primary School ensure that their curriculum includes literature from a wide range of authors, representing different cultures, backgrounds and experiences. This exposes pupils to diverse perspectives and helps to challenge the dominance of white, Western narratives.

2 They encourage critical discussions about the texts, focusing on themes of power, privilege and inequality. Pupils are taught to critically analyse how language can perpetuate or challenge stereotypes and biases. Speaking and listening is one of the Franciscan fundamentals that underpin their teaching and learning approach. Pupils are explicitly taught how to communicate within the discipline, using similar 'Speak like a poster...' to the ones created by LEO Academy Trust.

3 Their curriculum is designed to include topics and issues relevant to diverse cultural and ethnic groups. This helps pupils from minority backgrounds to see themselves reflected in the material and fosters a sense of belonging.

4 They create opportunities for pupils to share their own experiences and perspectives through personal writing tasks, class discussions and projects.

5 Their staff engage in ongoing professional development to stay informed about best practices for teaching in a diverse classroom, including culturally responsive teaching and anti-racist pedagogy.

Franciscan fundamentals

At Franciscan Primary School, their teaching approach is guided by the Franciscan Fundamentals – evidence-based strategies developed through research and collaborative practice. These fundamentals are designed to support accelerated progress and effective learning, particularly in enhancing disciplinary literacy.

In the classroom, you will see...

Adaptive teaching

By adapting teaching to meet diverse pupil needs, they ensure that all learners can engage with complex texts and concepts relevant to different subjects. Scaffolding, through visual aids and structured prompts, helps pupils grasp and articulate subject-specific language and concepts, promoting deeper understanding and application in their writing. Flexible grouping enables targeted support and collaborative opportunities, enhancing students' ability to analyse and discuss content in ways that build their literacy skills within specific disciplines.

Adaptive teaching strategies:

- flexible grouping
- explicit instruction
- metacognition
- scaffolding
- assistive technology.

Speaking and listening

Effective communication skills are integral to mastering disciplinary literacy. Their focus on speaking and listening supports pupils in articulating their understanding of subject-specific content and engaging in scholarly discussions. Through strategies like discussion statements, sentence stems and public speaking opportunities, pupils

Case study example: promoting inclusive and equitable disciplinary literacy

practise using academic language and structuring their thoughts in a disciplined manner. Harkness models and summary bullseyes further encourage critical thinking and vocabulary use, essential for writing and discussing disciplinary topics. Talk detectives ensure that discussions remain focused and productive, reinforcing literacy skills in a contextualised setting.

Continuous assessment for learning

Regular, formative feedback is vital for developing disciplinary literacy. By using questioning to assess understanding and providing specific feedback, they help pupils refine their use of academic language and improve their writing skills. Clear guidance on what constitutes successful work in various subjects supports pupils in meeting disciplinary standards. Encouraging peer and self-assessment promotes a deeper engagement with disciplinary conventions and expectations, allowing pupils to improve their literacy through reflection and critique.

Metacognition

The Education Endowment Foundation's 'Seven-Step Model' for Metacognition (Quigley et al, 2021b) supports disciplinary literacy by encouraging independent learning and self-regulation. Through structured curriculum planning and the gradual release of responsibility ('I do, we do'), this enables explicit teaching across the curriculum. Retrieval practice and feedback with clear next steps help reinforce knowledge and skills, ensuring that pupils can apply their learning effectively in disciplinary contexts. Technology is used to enhance understanding and engagement, further supporting literacy development.

Reflection

Reflective practice ensures that teaching strategies effectively support disciplinary literacy. Teachers engage in self-assessment and explore new methods to improve their practice, which directly impacts pupils' literacy development. Through lesson studies and reflective discussions, educators share insights and refine their approaches to teaching disciplinary content, enhancing their ability to support pupils in mastering literacy within specific subjects.

Monitoring and evaluation

Their monitoring and evaluation processes are designed to ensure that teaching supports disciplinary literacy effectively. By conducting learning walks, reviewing marking and feedback, and holding pupil progress meetings, they assess how well their strategies enhance students' ability to engage with and write about disciplinary content. Input from the school council and analysis of pupil voice provide additional insights into how well their approaches are working and where adjustments may be needed to support literacy development.

At Franciscan Primary School, their commitment to promoting inclusive and equitable disciplinary literacy has changed their educational environment. They prepare their pupils to become informed, empathetic and socially responsible citizens. Franciscan's data-driven approach and continuous reflection on teaching practices ensure that they meet the needs of their diverse student body, creating a supportive and enriching learning experience for all.

Further reading

Ball, R. & Fairlamb, A. (2025) *The Scaffolding Effect: Supporting All Students to Succeed. The Teacher Academy.* Routledge.

Education Endowment Foundation (2021). Special Education Needs in Mainstream Schools: Guidance Report. https://educationendowmentfoundation.org.uk/education-evidence/guidance-reports/send (Accessed: 04/04/25)

Durrant, G. (2024) *SEND Strategies for the Primary Years: Practical Ideas and Expert Advice to Use Pre-diagnosis.* Bloomsbury Publishing.

Quigley, A., Muijs, D. & Stringer, E. (2021b) Metacognition and Self-Regulated Learning: Guidance Report. Education Endowment Foundation. https://d2tic4wvo1iusb.cloudfront.net/production/eef-guidance-reports/metacognition/EEF_Metacognition_and_self-regulated_learning.pdf?v=1724004610 (Accessed: 04/04/25)

Wilkinson, S. (2025) Disciplinary literacy: excellence and equity across the curriculum. White paper https://media.hachettelearning.com/medialibraries/hodder/images-and-documents/whitepapers/2025-disciplinary-literacy-white-paper.pdf (Accessed: 20/05/2025)

References and bibliography

Bernstein, B. (2000) *Pedagogy, Symbolic Control and Identity: Theory, Research and Critique*. Revised edn. Rowman and Littlefield Publishers.

Bernstein, B. (2003) *The structuring of pedagogic discourse: class, codes and control, Volume IV*. Routledge.

Brock, C. H., Goatley, V. J., Raphael, T. E., Trost-Shahata, E., & Weber, C. M. (2014) *Engaging Students in Disciplinary Literacy, K-6: Reading, Writing, and Teaching Tools for the Classroom*. Teachers College Press.

Burke, P. and Kennedy, E. (2024) "Why Do You Think That?" Exploring disciplinary literacy in elementary science, history and visual arts. *Read Teach*, 77, 642–652.

Colwell, J. (2019) Selecting texts for disciplinary literacy instruction. *The Reading Teacher*, 72(5), 631–637, doi:10.1002/trtr.1762.

Counsell, C. (2018). Blog. Senior Curriculum Leadership 1: The indirect manifestation of knowledge: (A) curriculum as narrative. https://thedignityofthethingblog.wordpress.com/2018/04/07/senior-curriculum-leadership-1-the-indirect-manifestation-of-knowledge-a-curriculum-as-narrative/ (Accessed: 04/04/25)

Clark, U. (2005) Bernstein's theory of pedagogic discourse: linguistics, educational policy and practice in the UK English/literacy classroom. *English Teaching: Practice and Critique*, 4(3), 32–47.

Clark, U. (2010) The problematics of prescribing grammatical knowledge: the case in England, in Locke, T. (ed.) *Beyond the Grammar Wars: A Resource for Teachers and Students on Developing Language Knowledge in the English/Literacy Classroom*. Routledge, 38–54.

Cushing, I. (2025) Social in/justice and the deficit foundations of oracy. *Oxford Review of Education*, 51(3), 396–413.

Deng, Z. (2022) Powerful knowledge, educational potential and knowledge-rich curriculum: pushing the boundaries. *Journal of Curriculum Studies*, 54(5), 599.

Gaunt, A. (2025) Listening Without Prejudice: What Kind of Talk is Taught and Valued in the Classroom? in Wright, T. F. (ed.) *The Politics of Speech Education*. Cambridge University Press.

Hirsch, E.D. (2003) Reading comprehension requires knowledge of words and the world. *American Federation of Teachers*, 10–44. Available at: www.aft.org/sites/default/files/Hirsch.pdf (Accessed: 04/04/25)

Hudson, R. (1992) *Teaching Grammar: a guide to the National Curriculum*. Basil Blackwell.

Ippolito, J., Dobbs, C. L. & Charner-Laird, M. (2024) *Disciplinary Literacy Inquiry & Instruction*, 2nd edition. Harvard Education Press.

Kara, B. (2024) *Diversity in the Curriculum*. Sage Publications.

McCartney, M. & Carter, R. (1995) Spoken grammar: what is it and how can we teach it? *ELT Journal*, 49 (3), 208–218.

Ortlieb, E., Kane, B.D. & Cheek, E.H. Jr. eds. (2024) *Disciplinary Literacies: Unpacking Research, Theory, and Practice*. Guilford Publications.

Shanahan, T. (2019) Disciplinary Literacy in Primary Schools. https://ncca.ie/media/4679/disciplinary-literacy-in-the-primary-school-professor-timothy-shanahan-university-of-illinois-at-chicago-1.pdf (Accessed: 04/04/25)

Williams, A.P. & Martinez, D.C. (2024) Centering Minoritized Voices in Disciplinary Literacy Instruction, in Ortlieb, E., Kane, B.D. & Cheek, E.H. Jr. eds., *Disciplinary Literacies: Unpacking Research, Theory, and Practice*. Guilford Publications.

Wolsey, T. D. & Lapp, D. (2024) *Literacy in the Disciplines: A Teacher's Guide for Grades 5–12*. Guilford Publications.

Chapter 3:
Subject-specific talk or 'disciplinary talk'

By the time children reach school age, they have learned the schemata common to conversation, which are relatively 'open' ones characterised by taking turns in responding to what partners say.

(Hillocks, 1986)

For this book, I will keep the focus on 'disciplinary talk' with reference to talking like an expert. In short, I could author a whole book on oracy alone, without even looking at reading and writing. The issue with oracy is that it means different things to different people. However, I will summarise the key components from recent discourse and signpost to research that might further support a focus on this area.

The term 'oracy' seems to be back in fashion! Throughout my career, it has varied from 'speaking and listening', 'talk for learning', 'spoken language', 'oral language' and 'oracy'. I am told that speaking and listening is not the same as oracy because it involves a social justice aspect, and the debate continues, but all of this is open to interpretation. A term that might be useful for the purpose of this book is 'disciplinary talk' or 'subject-specific talk', where the focus concentrates on talking in a subject-specific way. This has also been referred to as, 'disciplinary oracy'. What I really mean is the focus on speaking and listening across the subject disciplines and how talk can help to facilitate this. In a sense, pupils learn to speak within the disciplines, e.g. learn what it means to speak like a scientist but also learn how discussion and debate can deepen their learning and develop their critical analysis skills within subjects. A focus on talk is not about policing language or disregarding the culturally diverse language that pupils bring to the classroom. All pupils deserve a language rich environment which enables them to excel.

The call for explicit teaching of speaking and listening has had a long history. The term oracy was coined by Andrew Wilkinson in 1965. Critiques of his work (Cushing, 2024) have mentioned that this focus upholds white middle-class values that minoritised certain groups. This book is not intending to alienate certain groups and is certainly focused on appreciating and reflecting the diversity of the UK and many other countries today. Many educators propose that code-switching (Wheeler, 2005) might be a way of navigating through this. Pupils will speak differently in different contexts. On occasion, they will be informal, through talking to friends or at home, and on other occasions, they may be formal, especially in job interviews or for primary pupils, when they are presenting in assemblies or school performances.

The key role of oral languages across the curriculum was documented right back to the Bullock report in 1975, where the call for oracy as well as reading and writing was raised. Reflecting on this decades later, the emphasis on talk across the curriculum remains a salient aspect of learning.

Here are some of the recommendations from the Bullock (1975) report:

- Exploratory talk as an important aspect of teaching and learning.
- Accepting pupils' accents and focusing on developing their language awareness and flexibility rather than suppressing their natural way of speaking.
- Providing opportunities for pupils to experience and use a variety of language styles, including formal and informal, to prepare them for different situations.
- Consciously developing pupils' listening abilities by creating opportunities within regular classroom activities.

Reference to disciplinary literacy:

- For secondary schools, the report emphasises that teachers should be aware of the reading demands of their subjects and provide support to pupils in meeting those demands. This might involve teaching subject-specific reading strategies, providing access to a range of texts, and helping pupils to develop their comprehension strategies within the disciplines.

Chapter 3: Subject-specific talk or 'disciplinary talk'

The strategies outlined by the Bullock report, all those decades ago, seem to have stood the test of time and are still a focus today as a way of improving standards across the curriculum. While communication, language and literacy are key components of the Early Years Foundation Stage and is present in our current curriculum, the primary curriculum has a few pages related to spoken language and reference to it in some other subjects, but it is not embedded throughout the curriculum. There should be more opportunities to cleverly weave this into the national curriculum.

Essentially, Oracy Cambridge and Voice 21 describe three examples of how talk can be utilised in the classroom:

- Learning through talk – the use of talk to deepen understanding.
- Learning about talk – the knowledge of spoken language.
- Learning to talk – the development of speaking and communication skills.

(Source: Oracy Education Commission. We Need to Talk: The report of the Commission on the Future of Oracy Education in England, October 2024.)

The Voice 21 and Oracy Cambridge oracy framework is incredibly helpful for demonstrating the vast aspects of oracy education for schools and for thinking about what this might look like across the different subjects.

It includes the following information:

1. Physical – these cover areas such as body language and tone.
2. Linguistic – for example, vocabulary and language.
3. Cognitive – reasoning, clarifying and summarising and the structure and organisation of talk.
5. Social and emotional – this is focused on working with others and the social aspect of talk, which could encompass the social justice element, where pupils feel like they have a voice.

Influentially, Alexander (2020) strongly advocates for dialogic teaching in the classroom, which might be placed within the cognitive aspect of talk. However, all four areas are interconnected. From multiple evaluations, 'dialogic teaching has been shown to increase student engagement and raises test scores in English, mathematics and science.' (Alexander, 2020 and EEF, 2021). Although there are various interpretations, 'dialogue is an exchange of ideas' and could be defined as a conversation, discussion, deliberation or argumentation.' Alexander (2020) focuses heavily on the types of questions that teachers can ask to elicit rich discussions that impact on learning. More recently, oracy has been a focus for organisations such as Voice 21, Oracy Cambridge, Oracy Education Commission and the English-Speaking Union. However, this book will focus on the disciplinary aspect of speaking.

Another key aspect of talk is exploratory talk, which might be necessary before accountable talk (explored shortly). Douglas Barnes introduced the concept of exploratory talk in his book, *From Communication to Curriculum*, which was first published in 1976 and later revised. He defined exploratory talk as:

... hesitant and incomplete because it enables the speaker to try out ideas, to hear how they sound, to see what others make of them, to arrange information and ideas into different patterns.

Participants engage in open-ended dialogue and discussion to develop their understanding. It might include:

- Hesitant and broken speech.
- Trying out ideas and hearing how they sound.
- Seeing what others make of the ideas.
- Arranging information and ideas into different patterns.

Following on from exploratory talk, a key aspect of disciplinary literacy is to require pupils to speak and think within a subject discipline and to use talk as a vehicle for understanding the key knowledge and skills they need to fully understand a subject. A fundamental way of doing this is to share sentence stems that model the ways in which pupils can begin to speak within the subject disciplines. It is also important for teachers to model their own thinking process which demonstrates how pupils might begin to speak and write like an historian, for example. Of course, as aforementioned, we are not expecting pupils to be speaking and writing like professional historians, but we are building rich schemata and preparing them for more formal essay writing when they reach secondary school.

Throughout this book, I have shared key language frames across each subject that support pupils with talking across the different disciplines. Wolsey et al (2024) state that 'a major component of disciplinary reading or close reading is to provide pupils with the opportunity to scaffold their disciplinary language and vocabulary in lessons.' They also argue

Chapter 3: Subject-specific talk or 'disciplinary talk'

that 'because pupils are typically novices in any given discipline…a useful way to support with the discipline of the language is through language frames' (also known as sentence starters or sentence stems). The language frames within this book endeavour to include academic vocabulary so that pupils can practise the language of the discipline. Indeed, they took me over two years to create because I wanted to trial them in classrooms and refine them, and they also explore nearly every subject. Some subjects required further training from subject experts to fully understand the disciplinary knowledge for each subject. These scaffolds are starting points for teachers, but they should be gradually removed after time or once the pupils become more confident at speaking across the disciplines.

Further reading

Alexander, R. J. (2006) *Towards Dialogic Teaching: Rethinking Classroom Talk*, 4th edition. Dialogos.

Davies, S. (2020) *Talking About Oracy: Developing Communication Beyond the Classroom*. John Catt Educational.

Gaunt, A. & Stott, A. (2019) *Transform Teaching and Learning Through Talk: The Oracy Imperative*. Rowman and Littlefield.

Gross, J. (2018) *Time to talk: Implementing Outstanding Practice in Speech, Language and Communication*. Routledge.

Knight, R. (2022) *Classroom Talk in Practice: Teachers' Experiences of Oracy in action*. Open University Press, McGraw Hill.

Mannion, J. (2023). Blog. Oracy Cambridge. The transformative power of oracy. https://oracycambridge.org/oracy-at-the-heart-of-the-curriculum/ (Accessed: 04/04/25)

Mercer, N., & Dawes, L. (2008) *Talk and Learning in the Classroom*. Sage.

Quigley, A. (2024). Blog. Disciplinary literacy: 50 years of failure. https://alexquigley.co.uk/disciplinary-literacy-50-years-of-failure/ (Accessed: 04/04/25)

Wolsey, T. D. & Lapp, D. (2024) *Literacy in the Disciplines: A Teacher's Guide for Grades 5–12*. Guilford Publications.

How can we compartmentalise our focus on disciplinary literacy?

Oral language can permeate across all subjects. It might be helpful to compartmentalise how schools think about their areas of focus when starting improvements in this area.

Teaching and learning strategy	English speaking and listening (and used across the curriculum) Transdisciplinary	Disciplinary speaking or 'talk' Speaking across the curriculum
Think, pair, share	Listening and responding	Speak like a... sentence stems
Cold calling	Reading comprehension strategies	Focussed talk time across the curriculum
Group work	Asking questions to extend, understand and build new vocabulary	Disciplinary questions
Metacognition: 'Think aloud', e.g. modelling the processes	Drama and role-play	Disciplinary reading
Questioning	Discussion and debate	Disciplinary writing
Feedback and formative assessment	Accountable talk: articulate and justify answers, arguments and opinions	Subject-specific speaking and listening skills
Peer discussion	Give well-structured descriptions, explanations and narratives for different purposes	
Collaborative work and the use of technology	Ask relevant questions to participate actively in collaborative conversations Speak audibly and fluently	
Addressing misconceptions, e.g. concept cartoons, using technology	Participate in discussions, presentations, performances, role play/improvisations and debate Gain, maintain and monitor the interest of the listener(s) Consider and evaluate different viewpoints Use appropriate registers for effective communication DfES (2014)	

Teaching and learning

As most teachers will notice, there are aspects of teaching and learning that already involve oral language and schools will find that they are already implementing most of it. This is positive as it means that schools can ascertain and prioritise the areas that need a deeper focus. Strategies such as, 'questioning', 'cold calling' and 'think, pair, share' are proven strategies that enhance learning and understanding for pupils, but also incorporate speaking and listening as a facilitator to deepen knowledge and understanding. All these need to be considered when implementing staff development on teaching and learning, so that schools can make links to speaking and listening within the strategies they use to teach pupils.

In addition, oracy can support meaning making. 'Effective Oracy practices in the classroom can activate relevant prior knowledge. By articulating thoughts, learners can clarify ideas, identify similarities and differences, and explore relationships between concepts, fostering deeper understanding' (Inner Drive, 2024). All these teaching and learning strategies are important for all classrooms.

References

Inner Drive (2024). Blog. The important role of Oracy in facilitating deep learning. www.innerdrive.co.uk/blog/oracy-deep-learning/ (Accessed: 04/04/25)

Further resources

Sherrington, T. & Caviglioli, O. (2020) *Teaching WalkThrus: Visual Step-By-Step Guides to Essential Teaching Techniques.* John Catt Educational Limited.

Watson, E. & Busch, B. (2021) *The Science of Learning: 99 Studies Every Teacher Needs to Know.* Second Edition. Routledge, David Fulton.

English speaking and listening

Back in 2003, I started an MA in education and my dissertation focused on how speaking and listening and process drama impacted on pupils' writing development. A key document back then was the DfES (2003) Speaking, Listening and Learning 'Lunchbox'. Which included timeless ways of developing drama, listening and speaking, especially within English but which can be used across the curriculum. My experience all those years ago, helps me to see the power of talk and how it can influence pupils' writing and understanding. Over two decades later and my thoughts remain the same. Speaking and listening can be used as a vehicle to support and underpin the curriculum, but it is not the panacea. Pupils need a balance of a range of strategies, including talk, purposeful feedback, vocabulary and explicit teaching. Here are some of the activities I have used for the past two decades.

Establishing rules for talk

Early in my teaching career, I learned that pupils need to have some guidance about speaking and listening, especially when presenting information. From reading and speaking to colleagues, I understand that there might be cultural norms or issues with expecting pupils to use Standard English when speaking. It is not my intention to disadvantage any groups of pupils, so these are just a few examples of what this could mean in practice:

- Clear speaking voice.
- Use intonation and expression.
- Take turns when speaking.
- Look at the audience when speaking (where appropriate).
- Look at the person speaking (where appropriate).

As a teacher, I always found it easier to co-create these where possible with the class through modelling what might be considered as less effective speaking, e.g. mumbling my words or speaking too quickly. We would then create class rules for talk.

Pupil roles

After many years in classrooms, I still believe that assigned group roles enable positive discussions and a focus for each pupil. Not every pupil is confident at public speaking, but they can take part in discussions and have valuable roles that can contribute to the discussion. Gaunt and Stott (2019) explain that 'discussion roles set out specific ways that pupils can interact with each other's ideas…and in turn raising the quality of talk.'

- Group leader/chair: This pupil makes sure the task is completed and organises the group.
- Scribe (note-taker): Writes down the main discussion points.
- Reporter: Works closely with the scribe to report the findings and summarise the key discussion points.
- Mentor: Supports all members of the group to carry out the task and explain any additional information.

- Observer: Focuses on how the group worked together and how each one contributed to the group.

Ideas in practice

Listening activities across the curriculum

Classroom technique	Explanation	Subject examples
Babble gabble	This game can be in small groups or whole class. The pupils listen to a short story. One pupil retells the story with as much detail as possible. When the teacher says 'Change', the next person needs to continue the story.	**English** Alternative way of retelling a story so that the pupils can use the ideas for their own writing. **History** Read some information on an historically significant person and then use this strategy to review and recall information about them. Use symbols to support recall.
Barrier games	Make sure the pupils have some sort of barrier, e.g. a large book or card. One person needs to give directions and the other needs to follow the instructions.	**English** Great activity to test whether pupils have written clear and understandable instructions. **Geography** Pupils could draw a map following instructions from their peers, based on a map of the school or similar.
Word tennis	Each person says one part of the story and the other must finish it so that it makes sense. For example: *one/day/a/princess/was…*	**English** Creating collaborative stories.

Classroom technique	Explanation	Subject examples
Ways to listen	This activity enables pupils to have different listening frames so that they can relay what they have heard. – Read a story and ask pupils to create questions they would like to know. – Pupils count how many times they hear key words or phrases whilst the teacher is reading. – Pupils visualise and create a picture in their heads as the teacher is reading.	**English** Create these opportunities after whole class reading.
All change!	This activity links to teaching fluency. The teacher says a sentence depending on the punctuation and pupils need to discuss how the punctuation changes the meaning of the word. E.g. Happy. Happy? Happy!	**English** An activity that will fit in with fluency activities where pupils are exploring their tone, intonation and expression.

Drama activities

Classroom technique	Explanation	Benefits
Freeze frames	Teachers can ask pupils to freeze at certain parts of the text that require further discussion. They can represent a certain emotion or a pivotal point in the text. This is usually accompanied with thought-tracking where a particular character comes to life and shares their thoughts and feelings at this point in the text.	Exploring and focusing on key parts of a text. Exploring character's thoughts and feelings. Looking deeper at certain parts of the text.

Classroom technique	Explanation	Benefits
Conscience alley	The teacher creates two lines – one might be the 'good' conscience' and the other the 'bad conscience'. One person walks along the line and each pupils says either a good or bad things. For example, if there is a section of a story where a pupil considers whether they should go in a house. *Pupil 1: You should go in; it might be nice and warm.* *Pupil 2: Don't go in because there might be horrible people.* *Pupil 3: It might have delicious food.* *Pupil 4: There might be monsters...*	This activity is great for exploring both sides of a problem, dilemma or discussion. It enables pupils to discuss their ideas before commitment to print.
Thought-tracking	Once pupils have frozen at key moments in the text, the teacher can choose pupils to share their thoughts, feelings or views.	Allows pupils to share the private thoughts of the characters.
Hot seating	This involves the class asking further questions to someone in role. This is almost like an interview, but the pupils need to be very familiar with the character and their motives and thoughts.	Focuses on the motives and thoughts of a particular character. This develops reading comprehension and supports writing in role.

(Adapted from: DfES (2003) *Speaking, listening and learning.*)

> **Speech and language difficulties: Five suggested tips for primary teachers from Maria Garcia, speech and language therapist**
>
> *'A key focus for talking to children with speech and language difficulties is to create a positive talk environment.'*
>
> 1 Repetition is very important for pupils as well as allowing them time to clarify questions.
>
> 2 Be aware of apprehension when pupils are speaking in a second language or in general. Making pupils feel comfortable is important for success.
>
> 3 Flexible grouping is very positive for these pupils.
>
> 4 Pausing and using non-verbal cues such as gesture, intonation and emphasising the important words are useful strategies.
>
> 5 Model new vocabulary and allow pupils to see your face and lips moving while saying a word or sound.

Accountable talk

Rather than passively absorbing the small body of knowledge the teacher is able to transmit, students can learn reasoning skills by talking and arguing their way through problems to conclusions and solutions. We and others call this type of structured discussion that supports learning 'Accountable Talk'.

(Resnik et al, 2018)

While we have general speaking and listening strategies which are applicable for all subjects and are of equal importance, as shown above, accountable talk is a very effective way of building dialogue, critique and debate within the primary classroom, especially for older learners. Other organisations have developed different names for this, e.g. Doug Lemov's 'habits of discussion' or a form of dialogic teaching. It gives pupils the opportunity of '…classroom talk to teach pupils to think—to make knowledge.' (Resnik et al, 2018). The table below demonstrates the key differences between speaking and listening and accountable talk in developing pupil's critical thinking skills needed to support today's world

Chapter 3: Subject-specific talk or 'disciplinary talk'

of social media and misinformation. It encourages pupils to justify their answers using evidence appropriate to the subject discipline, so that they are prepared for reasoned and evidence-based debates. This enables pupils to generate new knowledge.

Differences between 'accountable talk' and 'speaking and listening':

'Accountable talk'	'Speaking and listening'
Structured talk focused on deepening understanding through debate and critical thinking and a respect for the community	Develop speaking and listening skills across the curriculum
Builds knowledge and develops reasoning through collaborative dialogue	Enhances confidence through spoken language
Focuses on teacher guided prompts, student to student interactions and talk norms	Involves presentations, discussions, role-play, drama and storytelling
Evidence-based reasoning	Broad development of oral language skills and development

Accountable talk is a structured way, created by Lauren Resnik and colleagues, for pupils to discuss key aspects of a subject and is based on the following framework:

Knowledge: ensure discussions are based on evidence, e.g. What is your evidence?

Reasoning: justifying answers or claims, e.g. I know this because… . This will also depend on pupils having sound knowledge of the subject.

Community: this focuses on respecting all views and making the classroom a safe space to discuss and debate. E.g. 'I would like to build on Sara's response…'.

Figure 3.1 Accountable talk

This framework encourages debate that is facilitated by the teacher with questions that prompt discussion, e.g. *'Do you agree with Priya? Why? Why not? Can you tell me more about that?'* This type of talk enables pupils to collectively build knowledge and deepens their understanding of the subject being discussed. This also enables pupils to '...make their thinking "visible" by asking them to explain their understanding or to elaborate on their statements.' (Resnik et al, 2018).

Please see the case study examples from St. Matthew's Research School and the Knowledge Schools Trust for how some primary practitioners are using this in practice.

Use of technology in communication

Debates and discussions about key questions and concepts do not always have to be face-to face and in-person. The emergence of modern technologies and apps enable dialogue to take place online, especially when giving feedback or collaborative working on a piece of writing. These might be alternative ways to incorporate pupils who are non-verbal or have a particular educational need. This is similar with disciplinary writing, it does not always have to be written down on paper, but could be communicated in whatever form is appropriate, e.g. through an online presentation or a podcast.

Colwell et al (2023) explore the use of digital technology in their paper on supporting elementary teachers with disciplinary literacy. They argue and affirm that:

Digital texts and tools in elementary disciplinary literacy-focused learning can support, structure, and serve to enhance learning experiences, afford individualized interactions with text and allow students to engage in the study of texts beyond their traditional reading levels.

This is an important element of supporting disciplinary literacy because it enables pupils to access texts, even if they are unable to read it. For example, at LEO Academy Trust, we use apps, which will read a text to a pupil if they are unable to. This gives pupils dignity in learning and enables them to access the learning of the rest of the class. Of course, they will have intervention to support them if they are at the earliest stages of learning to read.

Disciplinary talk

Just as the science student must learn how to support a hypothesis with empirical data, a student of history should practice explaining and interpreting historical events from multiple sources of evidence. Because each discipline has its own genre of talk and criteria for evaluating sound arguments, students need opportunities to observe and practice these various forms.

(Resnik et al, 2018)

Taking part in speaking and listening activities across the curriculum and using 'accountable talk' requires pupils to have deep disciplinary knowledge (subject-specific skills) of their subject. If pupils are to reason, debate and elaborate on their answers, then they need to understand how each discipline carries out discussions and debates. The notion of subject specific debate is also echoed in the Oracy Education Commission Report (2024), where being able to shape an argument or solve a problem should enable teachers to, 'foster discipline specific ways of thinking and knowing', where pupils can draw on specific vocabulary and establish the different ways of interacting across the disciplines.

The table below exemplifies the types of sentence stems that might be used to promote discussions and the types of evidence that pupils might draw on to justify their claims. It is not an exhaustive list and only seeks to demonstrate what it could look like as a starting point for KS2 pupils.

Subject	Example sentence stems – pitched for KS2 (see each subject section for sentence stems across the age groups)	Evidence that pupils might use to justify their views
English reading	This text is linked to… I think that [word/ phrase] means… because… I think that…because… This section/text was about… because it says…	Quotes/ references from the text – *'I think that she is unhappy because it says she huddled nervously in the corner.'* Actions of the characters Facts, statistics and data Wider reading of texts with similar themes.
Mathematics	I know this because… My hypothesis is… The most efficient method would be… because… This problem can be solved by… This is important for real-life because…	Calculations Graphs, symbols or shapes Building on declarative knowledge, e.g. number bonds to ten, angles on a straight line multiplying by 10, 100 and 1000. *'I know this because 5x10 is 50, so 50 x 10 is 500.'* Checking calculations
Science	I have used this scientific equipment because… This is a fair test because…I predict that… The results show that/are reliable because… I have concluded that… My explanation is… The relationship is…	Data Observations Analysis Conclusions
History	They are similar/different because… This person is significant because… This has changed over time because… This source tells us that…because… Historians have interpreted this as… The consequence of this is…	Sources: letters, texts, diaries, artefacts, newspaper articles, photos, interviews, paintings, songs etc. Providing examples from multiple sources
Geography	The facts I have gathered tell me that… From undertaking fieldwork, I have observed that… This place is affected by human activity because… This physical/human characteristic is similar/ different because… From analysing…I've come to the conclusion that…	Maps, atlases, pictures, globes, sketches, statistics and digital/ computer mapping, texts, factual films etc. Observations, analysis, fieldwork Human values and attitudes Personal geographical experiences

Subject	Example sentence stems – pitched for KS2 (see each subject section for sentence stems across the age groups)	Evidence that pupils might use to justify their views
Art	I reviewed and developed my artwork by… The artist that inspired me was…because	Reviewing photos/ paintings Texts Knowledge of techniques
DT	My research has helped with this design because… I have selected these tools/materials because… My analysis and evaluation of this product is… because…	Product review Research into materials/ product
Music	I like/dislike this genre of music because… This composer/musician inspired me because… The lyrics in this song are about/remind me of…	Knowledge of songs Knowledge of composition Knowledge of musicians
RE	This artefact/text/story teaches us …about this religion… This text tells me that this [religious group] believes that… Many people in this religious group would do…in this situation…I would do this… because	Artefacts, religious stories, narratives, texts, pictures Personal experiences Aspects of living religion (such as rituals and cultural artefacts) Codified beliefs Arguments Case studies
PSHE	I think that…because… I would like to challenge that because … I would like to build on… I feel happy/sad/angry/worried because… I am responsible because… I show kindness to others by… I overcame this challenge by… I learn from my mistakes and never give up. I have listened to [XXX] perspective I am considerate of others when… I agree with your point…I would like to build on…I would like to challenge… I disagree because…	Personal experiences Experiences of others Texts

What could accountable talk look like in Early Years or Year 1?

The EEF's 'Preparing for Literacy' is a useful document that has clear strategies for improving talk in the Early Years. A way of improving early reasoning skills is to introduce key questions that probe reasoning skills. The pupil below read a text about a nurse called Emily who helps people in hospital. Giving a counterfactual reason is a strong way of developing early critical thinking skills.

Question type	Example – using people who help us With responses from a 5-year-old Reception pupil
Evidence	How do you know that nurses are important? What did she do? 'She helped Emily'
Reasons/theory	Why did the nurse help the woman? 'Because she had a bad cough.'
Counterfactual suggestion	What would have happened if the nurse did not help the woman? 'She will not be nice. She will tell everyone that the nurse is not helping her.'
Future suggestion	Who else could the nurse help in the future? 'She could help a daddy, mummy, doctor, brother and sister.' 'She can help your own baby.'

(Taken from Education Endowment Foundation (2018) 'Preparing for Literacy'. Adapted from Taggart et al. (2005) *Thinking Skills in the Early Years*.)

Case study example:
oracy and disciplinary literacy at Key Stage 1: Cheam Park Farm Primary Academy (part of LEO Academy Trust) with Giorgia Dibenedetto

Giorgia Dibenedetto: Key Stage 1 classroom teacher

Principal and vice principal: Craig Hudson and Emma Potter

Trust curriculum lead: Shareen Wilkinson

Talk is the most powerful tool of communication in the classroom and it's fundamentally central to the acts of teaching and learning.

(Professor Frank Hardman)

Giorgia is a KS1 classroom teacher at Cheam Park Farm Primary Academy and is passionate about improving oracy within her classroom. The approaches shown in this case study are because of a whole school focus on disciplinary literacy and oracy. Disciplinary writing takes place every half term for geography, science and history in Year 2. Science writing is completed in science lessons and geography and history disciplinary writing take place during the time when the pupils would normally be doing English in the morning, so that the quality of writing is high.

What knowledge and research supported Giorgia's focus?

- English speaking union focus on the 4Cs for the 21st century, which include communication, creativity, critical thinking and collaboration.
- Disadvantaged pupils are 2.3 times more likely to be identified as having speech, language and communication needs than those in more affluent areas (The Communication Trust).
- In many parts of the country, over 50 per cent of pupils start school lacking vital oracy skills (The Communication Trust).
- A focus on oral language skills is especially important for the development of a range of reading and writing skills in Key Stages 1 and 2 (Oracy APPG).
- The UK's poorest pupils start school 19 months behind their wealthier peers in language and vocabulary (National Literacy Trust).
- Pupils aged 5–9 years old are struggling to make friends because they lack self-confidence when speaking to others.

What key aspects of talk are within the classroom?

1. Using sentence stems to support discussions in the classroom (Figure 3.2).

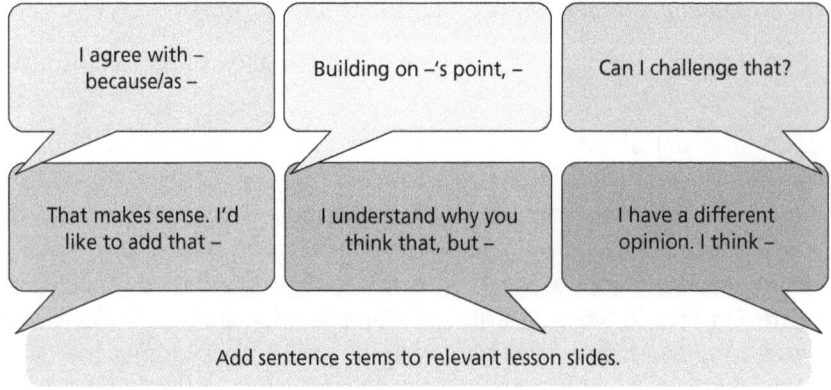

Figure 3.2 Discussion sentence stems

2 Use high quality non-fiction to read aloud to pupils and to introduce key concepts across the subject disciplines. Ensure that non-fiction texts, particularly those that link to topics studied, are displayed prominently in your book corner and are used for read aloud sessions.

3 Explicitly teaching new vocabulary across the curriculum and discussing key grammar aspects to link to English. A wonderful book to encourage vocabulary teaching is *The Word Collector* by Peter Reynolds.

4 Use of 'Speak like a...' posters on lesson slides and usage modelled by the teachers (Fig 3.3).

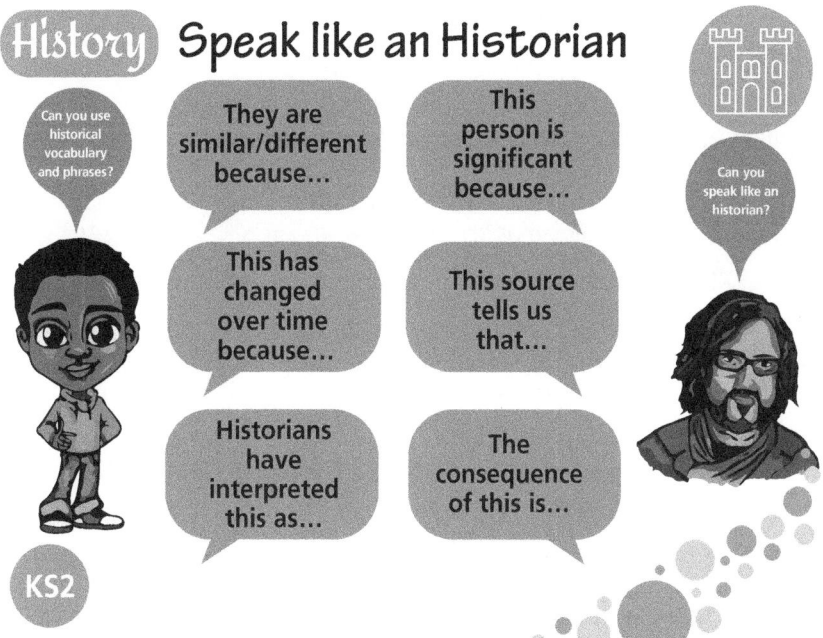

Figure 3.3 Speak like an historian

(Source: 'Speak like a...' posters created by Shareen Wilkinson and designed and drawn by Julaan Govier)

5 Use of talk groups to support group work and collaboration. This involves assigning roles to make to talk time purposeful and engaging.

6 Use of disciplinary talk time to improve disciplinary writing. This enables pupils to discuss their writing before committing it to print.

All these strategies have supported oracy in the primary classroom and have increased the quality of disciplinary writing.

References and bibliography

Alexander, R. J. (2006) *Towards Dialogic Teaching: Rethinking Classroom Talk* (4th ed.) Dialogos.

Barnes, D. R. (1976) *From Communication to Curriculum*. Penguin Education.

Bullock, A. (1975) A language for life. Report of the Committee of Enquiry appointed by the Secretary of State for Education and Science under the Chairmanship of Sir Alan Bullock F.B.A. www.education-uk.org/documents/bullock/bullock1975.html. Her Majesty's Stationary Office: London (Accessed 04/01/2025)

Carter, R. (2004) *Introducing the Grammar of Talk*. Qualifications and Curriculum Authority.

Colwell, J. (2019) Selecting texts for disciplinary literacy instruction. *The Reading Teacher*, 72(5), 631–637.

Education Endowment Foundation (2018) *Preparing for Literacy: Improving Communication, Language and Literacy in the Early Years*. Education Endowment Foundation.

Education Endowment Foundation (2021) Oral language intervention. https://educationendowmentfoundation.org.uk/education-evidence/teaching-learning-toolkit/oral-language-interventions (Accessed 04/01/2025)

Gaunt, A. & Stott, A. (2019) *Transform Teaching and Learning Through Talk: The Oracy Imperative*. Rowman and Littlefield.

Goldman, S. R., Britt, M. A., Brown, W., Cribb, G., George, M., Greenleaf, C., Lee, C. D., Shanahan, C., & Project READI (2016). Disciplinary literacies and learning to read for understanding: A conceptual framework of core processes and constructs. *Educational Psychologist*, 51, 219–246.

Hillocks, G. (1986) *Research on Written Composition*. National Council of Teachers of English.

Hudson, R. (1992) *Teaching Grammar: a Guide to the National Curriculum*. Basil Blackwell.

McCartney, M. & Carter, R. (1995) Spoken grammar: what is it and how can we teach it? *ELT Journal*, 49(3), 208–218.

Mercer, N., & Dawes, L. (2008) *Talk and Learning in the Classroom*. Sage.

Michaels, S., O'Connor, C. & Williams-Hall, M. C., with Resnick, L. B. (2010) *Accountable Talk Sourcebook: For classroom conversation that works*. Institute for Learning, University of Pittsburgh.

Moje (2008). Foregrounding the disciplines in secondary literacy teaching and learning: A Call for Change. *Journal of Adolescent & Adult Literacy*, 52(2).

Oracy Education Commission (2024). We Need to Talk: The Report of the Commission on the Future of Oracy Education in England October 2024. https://oracyeducationcommission.co.uk/wp-content/uploads/2024/10/We-need-to-talk-2024.pdf (Accessed 04/01/2025)

Quigley, A. (2018) *Closing the Vocabulary Gap*. Routledge.

Quigley, A. & Coleman, R. (2021a) Improving Literacy in Secondary Schools: Guidance Report. Education Endowment Foundation. https://d2tic4wvo1iusb.cloudfront.net/production/eef-guidance-reports/literacy-ks3-ks4/EEF_KS3_KS4_LITERACY_GUIDANCE.pdf?v=171249170 (Accessed 04/01/2025)

Resnick, L., Asterhan, C. & Clarke, S. (2018) Accountable Talk: Instructional dialogue that builds the mind. International Bureau of Education. www.researchgate.net/publication/324830361_Accountable_Talk_Instructional_dialogue_that_builds_the_mind (Accessed 04/01/2025)

Shanahan, C., Shanahan, T. & Misichia, C. (2011) Analysis of expert readers in three disciplines: History, mathematics, and chemistry. *Journal of Literacy Research*, 3, 393–429.

Shanahan, T. (2019) Disciplinary Literacy in Primary Schools. https://ncca.ie/media/4679/disciplinary-literacy-in-the-primary-school-professor-timothy-shanahan-university-of-illinois-at-chicago-1.pdf (Accessed 04/01/2025)

Taggart, G. , Ridley, K., Rudd, P. & Benefield, P. (2005) Thinking Skills in the Early Years: A Literature Review. Set: Research Information for Teachers. DOI: 10.18296/set.0525. www.researchgate.net/publication/265069159_Thinking_Skills_in_the_Early_YearsA_Literature_Review (Accessed 04/01/2025)

Wheeler, R. (2005) Code-switching to teach Standard English. *English Journal*, 94(5), 108–112.

Wilkinson, A. (1965) Influences on oracy. *Educational Review*, 17(4), 40–57. https://doi.org/10.1080/0013191770170401c (Accessed 04/01/2025)

Wilkinson, A. M. (1968) The implications of oracy. *Educational Review*, 20(2), 123–135.

Chapter 4:
English

Reading high quality texts in every subject, for example those that effectively illustrate the conventions of types of writing, gives students an opportunity to observe the discipline-specific aspects of writing that relate to particular subjects.

(Quigley et al, 2021a)

In the primary years, it is essential that young pupils grasp the essence and subject discipline of English before embarking on the specialised ways that historians, geographers and scientists write. English is its own unique discipline and if this is taught well, it paves the way for the other subjects. As mentioned, EYFS and KS1 pupils need to be able to compose a sentence orally and write a well-formed sentence – their foundational knowledge is essential and should take priority. Disciplinary literacy also enables pupils to apply generic literacy skills (e.g. capital letters and full stops) across the curriculum. Indeed, pupils can draw on their curriculum knowledge to write diaries and letters in English. For example, their own version of the diary of Anne Frank in English lessons. This chapter will start with the important skill of reading, before focusing on the key differences between reading and writing across the curriculum.

Although there are generalised ways that we read, for the purpose of disciplinary literacy, reading a text could mean reading fiction, non-fiction, poetry, a map, a picture, an artefact, an online article, a graph, a painting, an image or a table, and so on. This is a salient point to note because pupils need to navigate a wide range of texts throughout their primary years.

Reading in English example language frames

Nursery and Reception (Taken from EEF (2018))	[What is that?] *I think that is…* [What do you think this story is about?] *I think this story is about…* [How do you think the character feels?] *I think this character is [happy/sad/lonely]…* [Have you seen this before?] *This picture reminds me of…* 'So that', 'because' 'I think it's…', 'you could…', 'it might be…'
Key Stage 1	This text reminds me of… (background knowledge) I predict that… (predict) I can picture… (visualise) I would like to ask/ I wonder why (question) I think that… because… (infer) This section was about… (summarise)
Key Stage 2	This text is linked to… (background knowledge) From reading this part, I predict that… (predict) From this description, I can visualise… (visualise) I would like to ask/ I wonder why… (question) I think that [word/ phrase] means… because… (clarify) I think that… because… (infer) This section/text was about… [three main things] (summarise)

These sentence stems are based on the research from the Education Endowment Foundation Guidance reports on improving literacy in EYFS, KS1 and KS2. They are the essential knowledge and skills that pupils need to achieve in reading and writing and can be used at the start or during a lesson to support with talk activities. For younger pupils in the EYFS and year 1, the teacher can use them to support their modelling of disciplinary talk. Importantly, it is crucial that these are scaffolded over time and are age appropriate as pupils move through the primary school.

Reading comprehension strategies

It has been well established that there are specific ways that competent readers read texts in general. For primary schools, a good starting point is the EEF guidance (Bilton et al, 2021) on 'Improving Literacy' and the Reading Framework (DfE, 2023). If we are to read competently in English, then pupils need to learn to read strategically. This strategy is often time-limited (pupils only complete this for a short amount of time), but it is particularly beneficial for those who need explicit examples and forms a subject-specific example of metacognition. Very often, these are referred to as 'think alouds' because the teacher should clearly articulate their thought-process.

Interestingly, there is a distinct difference between reading comprehension questions and reading comprehension strategies. The first one involves a set of questions that pupils typically answer at the end of reading a text. The latter is focused on the strategies that competent readers use before reading, in the moment of reading and after reading. Not all pupils will need this to be made explicit, but it is especially beneficial for pupils with special education needs or those that need more direct and explicit modelling.

Whenever I complete training on the KS2 reading test paper, I always explore the reading comprehension strategies first, before looking at the different types of questions. Interestingly, sometimes we underestimate the power of visualisation when reading texts, especially for those who find reading challenging. Look at this question from the 2017 KS2 reading test paper (Figure 4.1):

35 Look at the paragraph beginning: *Carefully, Michael leaned….*

Where was the whale?

Tick **one**.

in front of the boat ☐

at the side of the boat ☐

under the boat ☐

five metres from the boat ☐

1 mark

Figure 4.1 KS2 reading test paper

(Source: Literacy Shed. Teaching resources. www.literacyshedplus.com/en-us/resource/2017-sats-reading-past-papers-en-gb. Published under Open Government License)

It seemed simple enough as a multiple-choice question at the end of the paper, but it required pupils to visualise what they have read. While 26.5% of pupils answered this correctly, but most pupils answered '*at the side of the boat'*. However, if pupils had imagined seeing, *'the whale's tapering tail on one side; on the other side the head with its scarred lines lay like a piece of huge dark wreckage'* (Standards and Testing Agency, 2017) they would have answered *'under the boat'*. Not only are they making inferences from the text, but they are building on their knowledge of being in a boat and visualising the situation.

For those of you not aware, the 2016 KS2 reading paper was particularly challenging for pupils and was discussed quite extensively. It required pupils to have extensive background knowledge and knowledge of complex vocabulary. The importance of reading and interpreting pictures can be seen in this paper. Equally, the reading comprehension strategy of being able to visualise what you are reading, also featured in one of the questions. These strategies work for reading a wide variety of texts and support pupils in the KS2 reading paper. This is shown in the example below (Figure 4.2).

8 which of these drawings best represents the monument?

Tick **one**

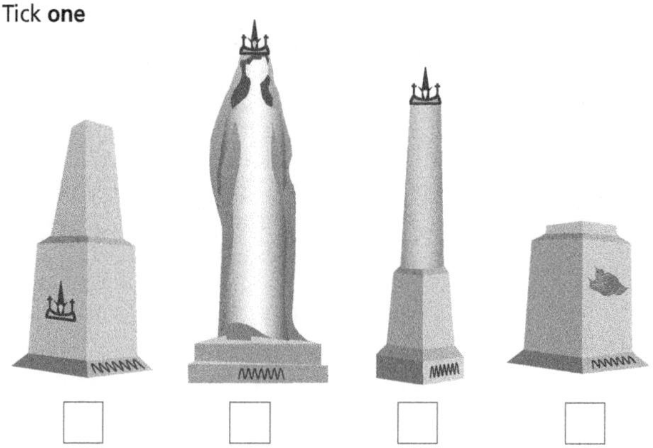

1 mark

Figure 4.2 KS2 reading paper

(Source: Standards and Testing Agency, 2016)

Both of these questions demonstrate how the reading comprehension strategies are still relevant to reading test questions. The tables that follow show how teachers could model the reading comprehension strategies across different texts types and different subjects through 'thinking aloud.'

Generalised ways of reading in English aligned with reading and analysing text types

Reading comprehension strategies	Make predictions	Visualise	Ask questions	Make connections/ activate prior knowledge	Clarify	Summarise
Narrative	Think about key characters and predict their actions	Read descriptions and imagine metaphors, similes and vivid language	Questions about characters' motives and actions	Connect to other characters and texts	Clarify the meaning of key vocabulary. Explore literary language	Five important things about the text
Recount – diary	Think about what key actions will happen next	Vivid descriptions of thoughts and feelings	Think about how the actions impact on the character	Draw on your own experiences	Clarify the meaning of key vocabulary	Five important events that happened
Information text	Look at headings, sub-headings, graphics and tables to make predictions	Understand what the table is trying to convey	Think about the key information. Decide which is important	Think about the topic and what you already know about it	Clarify Tier 3 vocabulary	Summarise each subheading. Use topic sentences to support
Poetry	Look at the verses, style and key words to make predictions	Read vivid descriptions and discuss what they are trying to convey	Ask questions about the vocabulary used and the rhythm, e.g. rhyming couplets and free verse	Establish the type of poem based on prior experience, e.g. Haiku, free verse etc.	Clarify the use of metaphors, similes and vivid language	Think about the key messages of the poem

Lent et al (2018) advocate the use of an 'I see, I think, I wonder, I connect', graphic organiser to support pupils with their disciplinary reading. It is a more pupil friendly approach to tackling different texts.

I think		I see	
'I think the character wants to...'		'I can see dark clouds hanging over the character.'	
I wonder	**?**	I connect	
'I wonder why that character made her cry.'		'This text reminds me of reading the text Tyger.'	

Disciplinary reading

Shanahan and Shanahan (2011) carried out some research on how historians, scientists and mathematicians read within their subjects, to ascertain the subtle differences between them. A summary of the research is provided below to exemplify the importance of understanding the subject disciplines. For primary pupils, this might be how the teacher demonstrates reading disciplinary texts to support all pupils with the differences and to discuss and ask questions.

Five key approaches that historians, mathematicians, and scientists use to read texts

Sourcing	Contextualisation	Corroboration	Text structure	Graphics
Historians: Use sourcing extensively, considering author's background, affiliations, and the nature of the document to evaluate perspectives and potential biases.	**Historians:** View contextualisation as crucial, considering the time, historical context and theoretical debates to interpret texts.	**Historians:** Use corroboration to evaluate author perspectives and biases by comparing texts and considering their own knowledge.	**All three groups:** Utilise text structure to support understanding and locate specific information. **Historians:** Additionally use text structure to analyse the relationship between narrative elements and the author's argument.	**Historians:** Claim to evaluate graphics like prose but didn't demonstrate it in the study.
Scientists: Use sourcing to select texts, considering author reputation and publication venue as indicators of quality, but don't use it for interpretation during reading.	**Scientists:** Consider the time to assess relevance, especially in rapidly changing fields, but do not use it extensively for interpretation.	**Scientists:** Compare texts for understandability and identify material differences in research methods and conditions.		**Scientists:** View different text elements as overlapping information that needs translation and comparison.
Mathematicians: Prioritise the content itself over the author's background, believing that the quality of ideas is evident in the work.	**Mathematicians:** Do not consider time or historical context, believing mathematical truths are timeless and independent of context.	**Mathematicians:** Use corroboration to minimise interpretive differences and identify established knowledge.		**Mathematicians:** Make no distinction between graphics and prose, interpreting them together.

Further reading

Hayes, F. Disciplinary reading. https://researchschool.org.uk/durrington/events/videos (Accessed 04/04/2025)

Durran, J. Disciplinary literacy: reading a challenging text. https://jamesdurran.blog/2024/08/19/disciplinary-literacy-reading-a-challenging-text-in-the-classroom/ (Accessed 04/04/2025)

Example

Look at the two texts below. How would you read each text?

| The remarkable journey of a plant begins with a tiny seed. When given the right conditions, this seed is stimulated to sprout. A root pushes down into the soil, anchoring the plant and absorbing water and nutrients. Meanwhile, a shoot emerges from the seed, reaching upwards towards the sunlight. Leaves then unfurl on the shoot, and with the help of sunlight, air and water, a complex process called photosynthesis takes place. This process allows the plant to manufacture its own food, enabling it grow taller and stronger. | A speck of brown, a promise green, The tiny seed, a hidden scene.

With warmth and wet, a magic spark. It wakes to life, breaks from the dark.

A hungry straw, the root dives down, Sipping deep from earth's brown crown.

A tiny fist, the shoot unfurls, Reaching high for sunlit swirls. Like emerald sails on a leafy mast, Leaves unfurl, the sunlight amassed.

A silent dance, a wondrous feat, Air and water, sunshine sweet.

The plants own kitchen, green and bright, Turns sun to food with magic light.

Stronger it grows, with each green tier, A silent giant, reaching higher. |

(Text created by Google Gemini)

Looking at the two examples above, the first one gives scientific information. If this were to be a text in the KS2 primary classroom, the focus would be on understanding the key vocabulary, with perhaps discussion or recall of the key terms. There might also be a diagram that

Chapter 4: English

complements this information so that pupils can visualise this in practice. Pupils need to build on their prior learning of plants and the plant life cycle, to comprehend and understand the text. In the second example, the focus is much more on understanding the vocabulary and the use of rhyming couplets to impact on the rhythm and flow of the piece.

Teacher tip: Artificial Intelligence (AI) is an excellent way of creating examples of different purposes of writing that can be used to demonstrate different text types and/or examples to use in the classroom. These will need to be edited and checked for accuracy.

Reading across the subject disciplines in primary schools – some examples of what this could look like

Generalised ways	Make predictions	Visualise	Ask questions	Make connections	Clarify	Summarise
Science	Make a hypothesis about what is going to happen. Think about the subject matter.	Use diagrams and pictures to understand key processes.	Discuss the key concepts and why they are happening. E.g. 'What helps the plant to grow?', 'How did you ...?', 'Why does this ...?', 'What makes me think that ...?','What do you mean by that ....?' (EEF, 2023)	Connect with previous science topics or other curriculum areas, e.g. mathematics.	Think about the key vocabulary and discuss their meanings.	In explanation texts, summarise five key scientific aspects, e.g. the plant life cycle or what materials conduct electricity.
History	Think about why a person is significant. Think about the time period.	Think back to the historical period. What can you see and hear?	Think about what is different or similar and what has continued or changed over time. Think about how historians have interpreted an event, e.g. 'What does this source tell me?'	Think about connections between events and draw contrasts.	Are there any historical words that need to be clarified? Who wrote or created this source?	Summarise the key events. Think about trends over time.

Generalised ways	Make predictions	Visualise	Ask questions	Make connections	Clarify	Summarise
Geography	Think about geography lessons in previous years to predict what might happen next.	Use maps, diagrams, globes and aerial photographs to understand geographical concepts.	Where relevant: 'Why is this place like this?', 'How is this place changing?' and 'How are other places affected?' (Ofsted, 2021)	Make connections with other subjects, e.g. science and mathematics.	Is there any geographical vocabulary that needs to be discussed and clarified?	Summarise the three things you have learnt.
Mathematics (Problem solving and reasoning)	Think about whether you have completed a problem like this before. What is the best strategy? Make estimates.	Write out the calculation. Use concrete, abstract and pictorial strategies. Use columns etc.	Has this improved my understanding of the question? Are there any other strategies I need to remember?	Does this link to other problems I have solved?	Check calculations.	Think about how well you have answered the question.
Art.	Think about the tools and equipment being used by the artist.	Think about what the artwork is trying to show.	Think about why the artist has inspired you.	Look at the background and history of the artist.	Clarify any aspects you are unsure of.	Summarise the three things you have learnt.

Generalised ways	Make predictions	Visualise	Ask questions	Make connections	Clarify	Summarise
Religious education	Have you read a text/book artefact like this before? Does this link to any other religious stories/texts?	Imagine the narrative in your head.	What does this teach us? How do this group view this situation? Why is this important to this religious group?	What would you do in this situation?	Discuss the meaning of unfamiliar words, e.g. 'resurrection'.	Write down three things you have learnt from this text/story.

Scarborough's Reading Rope (2001) also provides the broader context of the complex aspects of reading texts. Therefore, disciplinary reading will be a key focus for KS2 pupils who have already mastered decoding texts, as we do not want to overload pupils with too much to learn. This reading rope demonstrates that the reading comprehension strategies are not the only way we read as reading depends on multiple factors, including being able to 'compare and contrast' and recognise emerging themes. However, I have focused on these strategies for the purpose of the book, to demonstrate how this can be subject-specific across the curriculum.

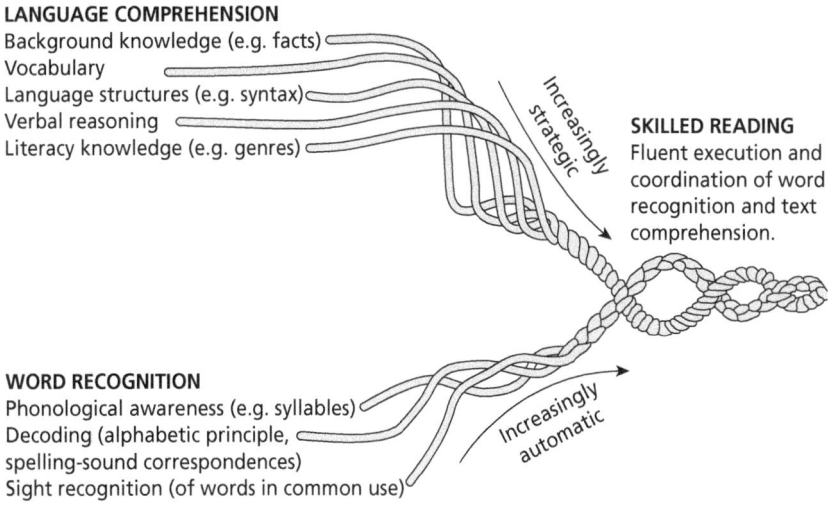

Figure 4.3 The many strands that are woven into skilled reading

Book talk

Another aspect of reading is to encourage book talk with pupils, especially to promote reading for pleasure. This is different to reading comprehension strategies because it promotes discussion after the pupils have read for pleasure and/or heard a story read to them. In Aiden Chambers' influential book *Tell Me* (2011), he advocates key questions that prompt discussion and talk about books. However, he does warn that pupils should not be given a list of questions and that these examples are for teachers to draw upon.

Was there anything you liked about this book?
Was there anything you disliked about this book?

Was there anything that puzzled you or you thought strange?
Were there any patterns – any connections – that you noticed?
Have you read other books like this? Is it the same or different?
Has anything that happened in this book ever happened to you?
What will you tell your friends about this book?

(Source: Chambers, 2011)

All these questions promote rich discussions for pupils to express and develop their understanding.

Stories across the curriculum

Stories are 'psychologically privileged'.

(Willingham, D., 2009)

Stories play an essential role in disciplinary literacy because they support pupils with their knowledge and skills of a subject and improve background knowledge. In essence, pupils will remember more of the content of their learning if it is within a story. Over 30 years ago, Graesser et al (1994) carried out a study exploring how much participants remembered from different types of texts. They listened to stories and then expository texts (e.g. non-fiction news articles, recipes, guides etc.). The results were quite profound:

Subjects listened to a set of stories and expository texts. Their memory was later tested and subjects remembered about 50% more from the stories than they did from the expository passages.

This important research has implications for the books we read aloud to pupils and the books we read across the curriculum. Stories are not only engaging, but they can also play a dual role in supporting pupils to understand key concepts. For example, the concept of empire and immigration could be understood through reading books like *Coming to England* by Floella Benjamin. If these books are deliberately sequenced, and tied to not just English but the curriculum, they support pupils with knowing and remembering more. The important role of stories is explored in further detail (with examples) in many of the interviews and case studies, including Cheam Park Farm Primary Academy, St. Matthew's Research School and LEO Academy Trust.

Further resources:

The Teachers' Collection. https://theteacherscollection.com/book-resources (Accessed 04/04/2025)

Case study example:
implementing disciplinary reading – an interview with Sonia Thompson and Hydeh Fayez

Sonia Thompson (Headteacher and director of St. Matthew's Research School) and Hydeh Fayez (Deputy Headteacher, DHT)

Background

St. Matthew's Research School is a one-form entry school in Nechells, Birmingham, England. It is a voluntary controlled Church of England School and has close links with the Diocese of Birmingham and St. Matthew's Church. The school has approximately 63% PP, 79% EAL and are above national averages at the end of Key Stage 2.

The school is expertly led by Sonia Thompson, who is a board member for the United Kingdom Literacy Association (UKLA) and the Education Endowment Foundation and was a part of the Oracy Commission. She is a trustee for Classics for All and the Church of England National Society.

The DHT of the school is Hydeh Fayaz, who leads on curriculum (including history, geography, oracy and phonics). She is an Opening Worlds project lead (a curriculum written by Christine Counsell and

Steve Mastin), part of the rethinking curriculum board for oracy and worked with Oracy Cambridge on oracy.

The school has been a Talk for Writing training centre since 2015 and supports schools with Sounds Write and the Exemplary Leadership Programme.

How did you introduce disciplinary reading and what does it look like now?

The big driver for the focus on literacy and reading started with the new curriculum in 2014. As a school, they were thinking about how they taught the foundation subjects. The knowledge and expertise from the subject associations was crucial to success and these supported the school to be clear about reading across the subject disciplines and the disciplinary and substantive aspect of each subject. Key vocabulary was built into teaching, and the reading aspect was fleshed out so that the expectations were made clear. The school created one-page guides for each subject and unpicked what the assessment would look like.

In 2016, Sonia attended a conference led by Doug Lemov, who was ground-breaking for how to teach reading. This is where the salient focus on reading in other subjects (disciplinary reading) and the importance of background knowledge truly came to fruition. It was at this moment that the school were introduced to the work of Isabel Beck and colleagues, and their work on Bringing Words to Life, through explicit vocabulary instruction.

Reading Reconsidered (Lemov, 2015) was used as a model for teaching reading, with a particular focus on close reading across the curriculum areas.

Close Reading is the methodical breaking down of the language and structure of a complex passage to establish and analyze its meaning. Teaching students to do it requires layered reading; asking sequenced, text-dependent questions; and should end whenever possible with mastery expressed through writing.

(Lemov, 2015)

Here is a summary of close reading:

- Close reading involves examining all parts of the text, including those that are easy to understand and those that are challenging.
- It's like taking apart a machine to see how its components work together. In a text, this means understanding how word choice, sentence structure and other elements create meaning.
- Close reading involves analysing the vocabulary, sentence construction and overall organisation of the text.
- Challenging texts: Close reading is most useful for difficult texts that require effort to understand.
- Establishing and analysing meaning: Close reading involves both identifying the main ideas and analysing how those ideas are developed and supported by the text.
- Effective close reading involves multiple readings of the text with different focuses, along with questions that require pupils to directly engage with the text itself.
- Pupils should express their understanding of the text through writing, which helps them develop strong analytical and communication skills.

(Close reading: https://teachlikeachampion.org/blog/close-reading-definition-close-reading/)

Transforming literacy through disciplinary reading

St. Matthews Research School prioritises encouraging a love of learning and deep comprehension in its pupils. Here's a glimpse into some of the key strategies transforming literacy in their classrooms:

- They emphasise a structured approach to story comprehension, using knowledge maps to help teachers and pupils develop a logical understanding of narrative elements.

Case study example: implementing disciplinary reading

- St. Matthew's believe stories can act as a powerful tool to bring the core curriculum to life. By prioritising engaging stories and using visual representations like illustrations or timelines, they aim to make learning more relatable and memorable for pupils so that learning becomes embedded into the long-term memory.
- Their teachers understand the importance of combining visual and verbal information (dual coding) to enhance learning. Vocabulary development is a key focus, with Tier 2 and Tier 3 words linked to curriculum topics and learned through interactive activities like word association games.
- The Opening World booklets and scheme serve as valuable resources, exposing pupils to a vast amount of vocabulary and subject-specific knowledge. The unit starts with a story, which pupils can explore and find out about the work of historians. For example, in the Indus Valley Year 3 unit, pupils read a story first before exploring the text through disciplinary reading questions. This approach encourages pupils to develop their disciplinary reading, such as reading like a historian or a geographer. It also enables them to remember more through introducing concepts through stories.
- St. Matthew's equip pupils with metacognition skills, teaching them to monitor their own comprehension. Sentence stems are one strategy used to guide pupils in reflecting on their understanding of the text. For example, before diving into a text, they facilitate discussions about the topic and the source itself. By 'following the thread' of the reading through discussions about the evidence and sources used by the author, pupils become more critical consumers of information.
- Pre-reading work emphasises source credibility. Pupils are encouraged to ask questions like 'Who created this?' and 'What was happening at the time?' to assess the strengths and weaknesses of the information presented. This critical thinking skill is particularly emphasised in subjects like RE and geography, where identifying perspective is essential.

Using stories across the curriculum

- Exposure to diverse texts promotes diversity across the curriculum by exposing pupils to a wider range of sophisticated texts that broaden their knowledge base and challenge them as readers.
- Reading books about events happening concurrently with a particular historical period ('meanwhile elsewhere') provides valuable context and supports pupils in making connections across time periods.
- They view reading as the foundational skill that underpins all other learning. It is the 'golden thread' that weaves together all aspects of their curriculum.
- Hinterland books serve a dual purpose: enriching the core curriculum with engaging stories and building key concepts within each subject area. Sonia describes this as, 'Oiling the wheels of the core.'

How often do you complete a piece of disciplinary reading? How is it organised?

- In history, geography and science they read parts of texts within all the lessons.
- If Year 1 were exploring animals – they would have a passage for them to read.
- Every foundation subject lesson has a small amount of the teacher reading aloud, echo reading and fluency development.
- Shared whole class reading – fluency elements.

What training did staff receive?

- This has taken years to embed and is not achieved overnight.
- Staff training has been ongoing, and this keeps the curriculum agile and flexible.
- Two areas per year so that it is embedded – real time to see this through.
- Focus on pedagogy – modelling is in every area of the curriculum.

- Two weeks – set targets – practice in our sessions. Use the EEF implementation guidance.
- Setting targets and revisiting the targets. Senior leaders model the process so that the improvement is supportive.

St. Matthew's essential tips for disciplinary reading and oracy

At St. Matthew's Research School, they're passionate about nurturing well-rounded learners with a deep understanding of their subjects. Here, they share some of the key strategies that have transformed disciplinary reading and oracy instruction in their classrooms:

- It all starts with a solid foundation. They ensure their teachers have a firm grasp of the key knowledge and vocabulary specific to each subject. This empowers them to curate texts that effectively build and reinforce these essential concepts in pupils. For instance, in history classes, teachers might focus on the vocabulary of source credibility, helping pupils understand how to evaluate the strengths and weaknesses of historical documents.
- They do not believe in overwhelming pupils with text for the sake of it. Their focus is on selecting texts with a clear purpose, ones that go beyond rote memorisation. By prioritising engaging stories and narratives linked to key concepts, they spark curiosity and make learning more memorable. This includes exposing pupils to real-world applications of disciplinary knowledge. For example, in geography, pupils might read about the Indus Valley civilisation, exploring the connection between the region's rivers and the development of Hinduism.
- Disciplinary reading isn't just about comprehending text; it's about enabling confident communication within each subject area. They actively encourage pupils to discuss the concepts they encounter in their reading. This not only reinforces learning but also prepares them to articulate their understanding effectively. After reading a scientific article, pupils might engage in discussions about the methodology used or the implications of the research.
- While a variety of texts can be valuable, they believe in being clear about the intended learning outcomes for each reading activity.

Text selection is deliberate, aligning with the specific knowledge and skills they want pupils to develop in each subject. For instance, in literature classes, teachers might choose a text with rich vocabulary to focus on word association activities, while a science class might prioritise a factual passage to hone critical thinking skills through source analysis.

- Subject associations are powerful partners. They utilise resources from relevant subject associations to identify high-quality texts and activities that support the knowledge they want pupils to retain.
- Weaving storytelling around key concepts is incredibly engaging. They encourage pupils to read texts aloud, then delve deeper by exploring the vocabulary and even creating new texts that build upon the themes and vocabulary introduced. Technology can be an asset here – exploring the use of AI tools to assist with text creation is an avenue they are curious about.
- Disciplinary reading is seamlessly integrated into their curriculum. By actively engaging with subject-specific texts, pupils organically build their knowledge base. For example, studying the Indus Valley civilisation might involve reading about the connection between the region's rivers and the development of Hinduism.
- They don't shy away from creating their own materials. Their teachers start by looking within the existing curriculum for opportunities to create or adapt texts that align with their learning goals. This approach ensures a smooth integration of disciplinary reading into everyday teaching practice.

Teaching writing and disciplinary writing

I have spent most of my career focused on improving writing in primary schools and there are a few strategies that have never failed me. Having worked on improving writing outcomes across the many schools, academy trusts and local authorities, my MA dissertation was also focused on improving writing through speaking and listening and drama.

Providing pupils with sentence stems, word banks and writing frames in English writing are powerful ways of supporting all learners to make rapid progress. All these tools are relevant for disciplinary literacy and can be used to adapt the curriculum. When writing in science, history or

Case study example: implementing disciplinary reading

geography, pupils will also benefit from having word banks and writing frames if they need them, especially those with special educational needs.

Research from Hillocks (1986) has stood the test of time and although there have been various iterations over the years, the information below still stands as some of the best-fit ways to improve writing and are still used in classrooms today.

Strategy	
Inquiry-based writing	This is especially helpful for non-fiction writing and disciplinary writing where pupil's need to use research and knowledge acquisition as a foundation for showing what they know and can understand. Pupils might gather information from various sources and analyse their findings through Accountable Talk (2010) before writing their pieces. Typically, pupils might start a piece of geography or history writing by being asked to answer an inquiry question, e.g. *Why was XXX significant?* Inquiry questions are not necessary for all writing, e.g. writing up science experiments.
Writing process	The writing process requires a continuous cycle of pre-writing, drafting, editing, revising, editing and publishing work. Pupils need to engage with each stage of the process and take part in peer and self-evaluation. This process can also be applied to disciplinary writing, where appropriate.
Explicit instruction in writing	Model and demonstrate the writing process to pupils through shared writing where the teacher can show how to generate ideas, organise information, develop coherent paragraphs and use effective vocabulary. These strategies can be modelled through guided practice with a focus on independent application. The Education Endowment Foundation seven-step metacognition model is appropriate here (Quigley, 2021b).
Collaborative writing	Enable a collaborative writing environment where pupils can share their work, provide feedback to peers and engage in collaborative writing tasks. This approach helps pupils develop critical thinking skills, learn from their peers and improve their own writing.
Authentic writing	Provide pupils with authentic writing tasks that connect to their interests and experiences. These tasks should have a clear purpose and audience, and they should allow pupils to apply their writing skills in meaningful ways.

The strategies above can be used when modelling and demonstrating disciplinary writing with primary-aged pupils. The only difference might be that the purpose for writing is slightly different. In primary English, there are four main purposes for writing: to describe, to narrate, to inform, and to persuade. The focus on audience is also important here because this will affect the register (vocabulary and grammar) that a pupil uses through formal and informal writing. In disciplinary literacy, the tone of the writing tends to be formal and academic, and the purpose of the writing is for pupils to show what they know and understand. They can, of course, draw on their English knowledge, but they are essentially displaying their disciplinary and substantive knowledge of a subject (where appropriate).

English writing example language frames

The language frames below were written based on what writers might think and say as they write. They are pitched to be appropriate for the age and stage of the pupils and are a metacognitive approach, based on the discipline of writing, as set out in the programmes of study for English writing.

Reception	I can read and hear lots of stories. I can say and write [a word/sentence]. I can use my sounds to write a word. I can check if my writing makes sense. I can use capital letters and full stops.
Key Stage 1	I have used [text/story] to inspire my writing. I have used this vocabulary because… The purpose for this writing is… I can think, say, hear and write a sentence. I can check that my work makes sense. I have edited my work by…
Key Stage 2	I have drawn on [book/text] to write this because… I chose this vocabulary because…the effect is… The audience and purpose for this writing is… I have maintained the reader's interest by… I can orally rehearse my writing. I have edited and proof-read my work by…

English grammar and disciplinary grammar

Another key link to English writing with geography, history or science writing is that learning about non-fiction writing links perfectly to disciplinary writing. This type of writing is likely to be more formal, academic and use features such as the subject-specific vocabulary or Tier 3 words, e.g. evaporation, condensation in science or take-away in mathematics. Pupils do not necessarily need to be made explicitly aware of the grammar of each discipline in subject lessons. At the Primary Knowledge Trust (see case study) they teach this explicitly in English lessons. In addition, at LEO Academy Trust, Year 5 pupils fed back to me that they wanted to, 'demonstrate their learning within a subject.' For example, showing their knowledge of the Roman Empire.

A feature is the use of the passive voice in science and geography and the active and passive voice in history. Indeed, this fits perfectly with non-fiction writing and enables pupils to develop their non-fiction writing across the curriculum. By the end of Year 6, pupils are expected to use and understand the difference between formal and informal writing and the key grammatical and structural features, e.g. headings and sub-headings. The information below will provide further details.

Active and passive voice explained

Active: *Shareen ate the biscuits.*

Passive: *The biscuits were eaten by Shareen.*

The subject (the biscuits) moves to the end of the clause and is no longer the subject but is the agent/object. It starts with the preposition 'by'.

Agentless passive: *Shareen (object/agent) ate the biscuits.*

The biscuits were eaten.

The agent (or object) is omitted from the sentence.

The agentless passive is seen in more formal writing and can be used to build suspense or to give pupils' writing a more authoritative style.

Understanding the features of formal and informal writing is essential when applying more formal examples to disciplinary writing. If pupils are exposed to this in English, then it paves the way to a more seamless transition in other subjects. The term 'less formal' is used deliberately, because sometimes writing can have a combination between the two and levels of formality are on a continuum.

Less formal	Formal
Contracted forms *They've made their way...* *Don't touch that!*	Modal verbs in certain grammatical structures *This country would appear normal...* *Most people believe that...*
Question tags *It's cold, isn't it?* *These are your pencils, aren't they?*	Use of abstract nouns and noun phrases *Consumers believe that...* *Inside this tiny package is a baby plant...*
'Multi-word' verbs, for example: *Go in* rather than *enter* *find out* rather than *discover* *ask for* rather than *request* (KS2 English grammar and punctuation appendix)	Passive *It was suggested that...* *Aina was captured...*
Passives using 'get', for example: *I got my new shows last week.* *He got told off by my mum.*	Vocabulary – context/subject-specific ...significance... ...producers... ...condensation... ...pollination....
Second person direct address to the reader *If you are reading, this is the book for you!* *Are you nervous about starting school?*	
Vernacular (everyday) language, including idioms *I had no clue what was going on.* *Just add a little bit of milk.* *I've been hanging out with my friends.*	
Features that replicate spoken language, such as: Ellipsis *'...You, okay?' 'Yeah.'* (Ellipsis here is of a word rather than building suspense. It might say: 'Are you okay?') Discourse markers *So, what would you like for tea?* Non-standard forms *'I wasn't doing nothin''*	

(Adapted from: Standards and Testing Agency Key Stage 2 moderator training)

Structuring sentences and understanding paragraph structure is key to developing writing and disciplinary writing. It is important to introduce a paragraph with a topic sentence and then to support it with details, before ending your sentence. In disciplinary writing, older pupils need to be able to support their writing with evidence and reasoning, drawing on their research.

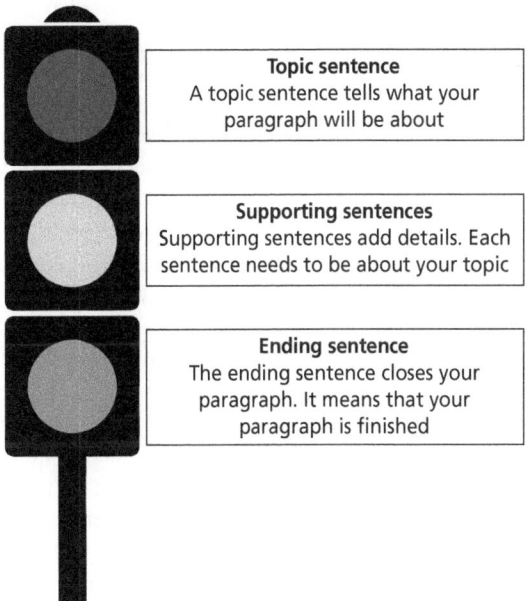

Figure 4.4 Understanding paragraph structure

An example of disciplinary science writing

The first stage starts with a seed *[Topic sentence. Introduces what the paragraph is about]*. Inside this tiny package is a baby plant, food to help it grow and a protective coat. The seed can stay asleep for a long time, even years, until the right conditions come along. When it's warm and wet enough, the seed wakes up and starts to sprout. A tiny root pushes out first, helping the seedling hold on tight in the soil. Then, a shoot grows upwards, reaching for the sunlight *[Supporting sentences. Adds the detail about the topic of the first stage]*. The first leaves, called cotyledons, appear and start making food for the growing plant *[Concludes the paragraph]*.

Further reading

Hochman, J. C. & Wexler, N. (2024) *The Writing Revolution 2.0: A Guide to Advancing Thinking Through Writing in All Subjects and Grades*. Wiley

Quigley, A. (2022) *Closing the Writing Gap*. Taylor & Francis.

Shackleton, J. (2017) *Grammar Survival for Primary Teachers: A Practical Toolkit*. Routledge.

Recommendations

- Remember, like other subjects, disciplinary literacy does not always have to have a written outcome. This could be oral or utilise technology to support pupils who need it.
- Schools can cover writing linked to history, geography and science etc. in English, but as research shows (Graham and Herbert, 2010), the act of writing helps to enhance pupils content knowledge, which in-turn supports reading comprehension.
- By KS2, pupils will not be able to fully write like an historian, geographer or scientist (in an age-appropriate way) until they have the knowledge of facts, dates and times and how specialists carry out their work. It needs to be completed after they have learnt the content.
- Disciplinary writing needs to be modelled, and the sentence structures made explicit to pupils. This can be achieved by reading lots of writing by historians and using (ideally) authentic texts where appropriate.
- It is suggested that a longer piece is carried out at the end of a unit of work (perhaps after six weeks of study), but this can vary from once a year to three times a year.
- Plan out and decide when and how often opportunities for extended disciplinary writing will be provided. In the case study schools, this varies from once a year to one piece of geography, history or science writing every term. Indeed, pupils will be writing, reading or engaging in oral discussions in nearly every lesson, this is more about extended pieces of writing.
- Have a key question in mind, so that it is explored over the weeks of study. For example, *'How did migration impact on the British Empire?'* That way pupils can build up their knowledge before writing.
- Information texts are vital for disciplinary writing and some schools call these 'double-page spreads', where pupils show what they know and understand about the topic, but they are not the only forms of disciplinary writing as shown in each subject chapter.

- Make connections with other subjects. The primary curriculum is packed and we are often struggling for time, so the more we can make connections the better.

Vocabulary – explicit and implicit approaches

Within rich reading and writing lies the important aspect of vocabulary. Essentially, explicit vocabulary teaching aims to instil in pupils a deep and nuanced understanding of words. As Lemov et al (2018) eloquently put it:

A primary goal of Explicit Vocabulary Instruction is to model for pupils the depth of knowledge that is involved in mastering words: to own a word is to know not just its definition but its different forms, its multiple meanings, its connotations, and the situations in which it's normally applied.

This means going beyond simple definitions. Pupils should develop a rich understanding of a word's various meanings and applications. While implicit methods like reading aloud and encouraging independent reading are vital, explicit vocabulary instruction – directly teaching new words – is equally crucial for language development. It's also essential to explore vocabulary across all areas of learning: reading, writing and speaking, and within various subjects.

Isabel Beck and colleagues (2013) are frequently referred to when discussing aspects of explicit and implicit teaching of vocabulary. Like all areas of teaching, vocabulary is not the only aspect that improves English and other subjects, but it is one that we might not have had as much focus on in the past.

Beck et al (2013) focus on the tiers of vocabulary and advocate that teachers should explicitly teach Tier 2 and 3 vocabulary. Of course, very young pupils might also benefit from explicit teaching of Tier 1 vocabulary if this is their need.

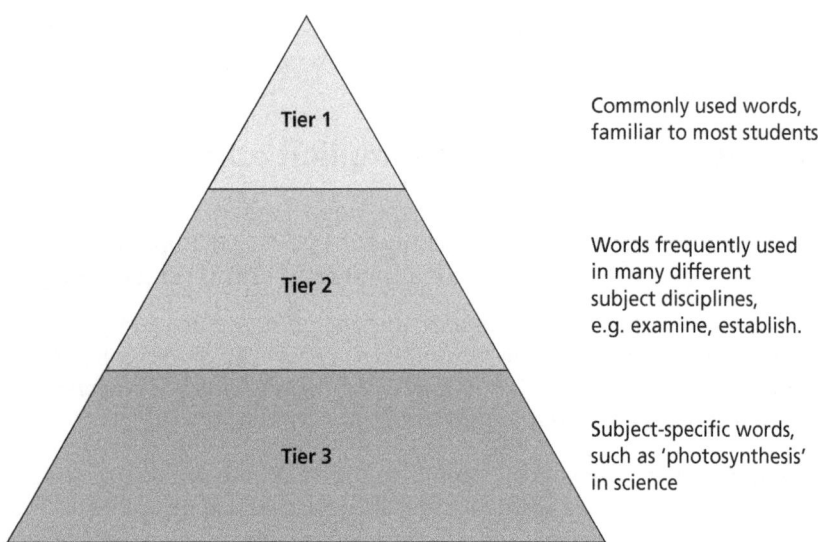

Figure 4.5 The three tiers of vocabulary

Shanahan and Shanahan (2014) express the importance of teaching the vocabulary not just from stories but also from non-fiction. These should be explicitly linked to the teaching of etymology, so that pupils understand the origins and roots of words. Indeed, words can have different meanings according to the context. For example, 'take-away' in mathematics, means something different to a 'take-away' on a Friday night. So, for older primary pupils, possibly from KS2, studying etymology can help them with understanding words. For example, the word 'port' originally comes from Latin. If we understand that it means 'to carry', then the words portable and transport are easier to understand if we know their origin. Vocabulary features heavily within the disciplines and understanding technical terms or Tier 3 vocabulary is crucial for success.

References and bibliography

Beck, I. L., McKeown, M. G. & Kucan, L. (2013) *Bringing Words to Life: Robust Vocabulary Instruction*. Guilford Publications.

Busch, B. (2024) The role of oracy in deep learning. Blog. www.innerdrive.co.uk/blog/oracy-deep-learning/ (Accessed 04/01/2025)

Chambers, A. (2011) *Tell Me (Children, Reading and Talk): With the Reading Environment*. Thimble Press.

DfES (2023) The Reading Framework. https://assets.publishing.service. gov.uk/media/664f600c05e5fe28788fc437/The_reading_framework_.pdf (Accessed 04/01/2025)

Education Endowment Foundation (2018). Preparing for Literacy: Improving Communication, Language and Literacy in the Early Years. London: Education Endowment Foundation. https://d2tic4wvo1iusb. cloudfront.net/production/eef-guidance-reports/literacy-early-years/ Preparing_Literacy_Guidance_2018.pdf?v=1724153990 (Accessed 04/01/2025)

Education Endowment Foundation (2023). Improving Primary Science: Guidance Report. https://d2tic4wvo1iusb.cloudfront.net/production/eef-guidance-reports/primary-science-ks1-ks2/improving-primary-science-guidance-report-ks1-ks2.pdf?v=1723581620 (Accessed 04/01/2025)

Graesser, A. C., Singer, M. & Trabasso, T. (1994) Constructing inferences during narrative text comprehension. *Psychological Review*, 101(3), 371.

Lent, R. C. & Voigt, M. M. (2018) *Disciplinary Literacy in Action: How to Create and Sustain a School-Wide Culture of Deep Reading, Writing, and Thinking*. SAGE Publications.

Oakhill, J., Cain, K. & Elbro, C. (2014) *Understanding and Teaching Reading Comprehension: A Handbook*. Taylor & Francis.

Ofsted (2021) Research review series: geography. www.gov.uk/ government/publications/research-review-series-geography/research-review-series-geography#disciplinary-knowledge (Accessed 04/01/2025)

Quigley, A. & Coleman, R. (2021a) Improving Literacy in Secondary Schools: Guidance Report. Education Endowment Foundation. https://d2tic4wvo1iusb.cloudfront.net/production/eef-guidance-reports/literacy-ks3-ks4/EEF_KS3_KS4_LITERACY_GUIDANCE. pdf?v=1712491708 (Accessed 04/01/2025)

Scarborough, H. S. (2001) Connecting early language and literacy to later reading (dis)abilities: Evidence, theory, and practice. In Neuman, S. & Dickinson, D. (Eds.) *Handbook for Research in Early Literacy* (pp. 97–110). Guilford Press.

Shanahan, C., Shanahan, T. & Misischia, C. (2011) Analysis of expert readers in three disciplines: History, mathematics, and chemistry. *Journal of Literacy Research*, 43(4), 393–429.

Standards and Testing Agency (2016) *Key Stage 2 Reading Answer Booklet.* The Stationary Office

Standards and Testing Agency (2017) *Key Stage 2 Reading Answer Booklet and Reading Booklet.* The Stationary Office

Willingham, D. T. (2009) *Why Don't Students Like School? A Cognitive Scientist Answers Questions About How the Mind Works and What It Means for the Classroom.* Wiley.

Further reading

Ashley, K. (2019) *Word Power: Amplify Vocabulary Instruction.* Singular Publishing.

Quigley, A. (2018) *Closing the Vocabulary Gap.* Routledge.

Chapter 5:
history

Historians strive—not for truth—but for plausible and coherent interpretations, and history reading requires an analogous set of processes.

Shanahan (2019)

Before embarking on the discipline of history, it is important to comprehend the different types of knowledge that pupils need to know and understand. It is also vital that pupils have a strong grasp of English, and that English is taught as a subject discipline in its own right. To write like an historian, pupils need both substantive and disciplinary knowledge. Substantive knowledge refers to the facts of the subject. Disciplinary knowledge refers to the subject-specific skills that historians need to acquire these facts. In short, how do we think, speak read, and write like an historian? A key distinction here is that these 'skills' are not generic but are clearly specific to the subject. It is recommended that pupils work towards answering a key inquiry question and disciplinary writing is a perfect way of demonstrating pupils' knowledge and understanding of their original inquiry question. For example, their writing would answer questions about why an historical person was significant.

However, after a few years of delivering training on disciplinary literacy, I have found that starting with subject specific 'skills' as opposed to 'disciplinary literacy' can be beneficial for understanding. We sometimes need 'a hook' if words or concepts are new to us.

Substantive knowledge (facts)	Disciplinary knowledge (how historians acquire the facts)
For example knowing facts and dates about: Mary Seacole and Florence Nightingale; Neil Armstrong; Ancient Greeks, Henry VIII, Great Fire of London; Roman Empire and the Ancient Greeks; the Benin Empire, the Sikh Empire etc.	For example historians explore: cause and consequence; similarity and difference; connections, contrasts and trends; historical significance and sources and evidence.

(Source: KS1 and KS2 National Curriculum in England, 2014)

For primary pupils, writing in history-like ways can be complex and challenging, especially if it is not explicitly taught to pupils. For KS1 pupils, this is not about large amounts of writing. It is also not about writing stories or diaries when the focus should be on non-fiction or information texts in history. It is about the quality and content of the writing. Shorter writing might provide pupils with a more grounded understanding of historical writing needed for KS2, than writing a letter from the point of view of Samuel Pepys which can be explored in English.

Look at these two KS1 examples on Mary Seacole. Which one is history writing?

- Mary Seacole was known as Mother Seacole, but Florence Nightingale was known as the Lady of the Lamp because of her work caring for wounded soldiers at night.
- [Diary of Mary Seacole] I feel extremely upset. I travelled all the way to London because I am so enthusiastic about supporting others. It is unfair because I know that I would do a brilliant job. I am determined to go – I will pay for the trip myself!

In the first example, the pupil is demonstrating their disciplinary knowledge of similarity and difference (through comparing Mary Seacole and Florence Nightingale). After studying both nurses, KS1 pupils are then encouraged to discuss and write about what is similar and different about them and should justify this with evidence. This requires historical knowledge of both nurses and knowledge that historians explore similarity and difference. It also draws on the English strategy of justifying answers with evidence from the text. The second example, which I would be happy to see in any Year 2 classroom, firmly demonstrates their English knowledge of the convention of diaries, through using the first person 'I' and explores Mary's thoughts and feelings. It should be clearly articulated that this is within the English discipline, perhaps in the English books, and is not history writing. Some schools do have the same book across English and the humanities, but we can still make the subject purpose clear to them. This is not to say that KS1 pupils cannot write diaries from historical characters – they can, but it needs to be made clear that this is English writing, drawing on their historical knowledge. In KS1 quality and not quantity is vital to understanding.

This concept was explored by Ofsted in their 2023 subject review: rich encounters with the past of history.

> In most schools, leaders had not considered how content choices in Reception or key stage 1 might help to prepare children with knowledge and vocabulary necessary for later study. For example, most schools taught about the great fire of London in depth at key stage 1, but leaders had not generally identified what knowledge pupils could develop from this topic that would help them later.

The core aspects of what historians do are understood as the following:

- Ask and answer questions.
- Use historical vocabulary.
- Note connections, contrasts and trends over time.
- Change and cause.
- Similarity and difference.
- Historical significance.
- Sources and evidence (including interpretations).

(Source: KS1 and KS2 history national curriculum and Ofsted research reviews)

Speaking and thinking like an historian - language frames

These language frames were written to support pupils and teachers with understanding how historians conduct their work (or with disciplinary knowledge). It was important that these sentence stems are made explicit from Nursery and Reception to build rich schemata.

Nursery and Reception (Prompts for adult modelling)	They are similar/different... This person is important... It has changed because... This happened on...
KS1	They are similar/different because... This person is significant because... This was caused by... This source tells us that... Historians have described this as...This has changed over time because...
KS2	They are similar/different because... This person is significant because... This has changed over time because... This source tells us that... Historians have interpreted this as... The consequence of this is...

EYFS

There was just one school where leaders took a wider view and specified important vocabulary and concepts, such as farming, which children could encounter in Reception, and which would help them learn specific history topics in the future. In this school, children were well prepared for what they went on to learn in history.

(Rich encounters with the past: History subject review, Ofsted 2023)

The EYFS is the base for everything to come. It is vital that teachers and leaders are aware of how the EYFS can support pupils with their future learning, while respecting and valuing their work in the EYFS. This is not about teaching KS1 aspects to EYFS pupils or KS3 aspects to KS2 pupils. This is about being deliberate and considered about how the EYFS can support history. For example, reading stories about kings and queens is a powerful way of starting the notion of power with young pupils. Below, we explore this in more detail.

Early learning goals

For those of you who are unfamiliar, and mainly teach in KS2, the early learning goal is the expectation for pupils to reach by the end of the reception year. Pupils in Nursery find the concept of the past challenging, but a small amount of learning will help them to prepare for the future. Stories and texts can introduce young learners to historical concepts where they can explore kings and queens and read about other worlds from the past. Pupils need to be exposed to a range of different texts that represent diversity and show a range of people. For example, *Coming to England* by Dame Floella Benjamin is a fabulous text about travel, but also begins to build the concept of empire and monarchy for young pupils.

Very often, I am met with trepidation when I mention disciplinary literacy in EYFS. This entails adults cleverly interweaving disciplinary questions and vocabulary through modelling in the learning environment and across all areas of learning, so that pupils are ready for more subject specific writing in KS1. There is also no expectation that primary pupils know and understand the terms substantive and disciplinary knowledge, but it is important that teachers know and understand the roles they play as pupils move through the primary years.

Examples	Adult modelling and questioning
They are similar/different…	'Can you tell me what is similar or different to the clothes your grandparents are wearing?' [Pictures] 'Do these cars look similar or different to today?' 'Wow, they did not have fast cars in the past.'
This person is important…	'The police and nurses are important because they help people.' 'Nurses are important because help you when you are ill.'
This happened on…	'This happened before you were born.' 'This happened when you were at home…'

KS1 and KS2

These sentence stems are to support teachers to model the language that historians might use and to support the development of disciplinary knowledge. It might not be until KS2 that pupils are independently accessing them to use in their own work. When historians are thinking and speaking, they are focusing on similarity and difference, thinking about various sources and how they help us to interpret the past, and crucially thinking about how historians have interpreted events.

In KS1, the sentence stems function as a starting point for building on learning in EYFS and starting the journey towards subject-specific writing in history. This does not mean endless pages of writing, but that the emphasis is on the quality and not quantity of the history writing.

Year 2 (KS1) example for teachers to model

Mary Seacole

Mary Seacole **is significant** because she showed that medical care could come from experience and practical skills and not just training.

This source tells us that Mary Seacole was from Jamaica.

Florence Nightingale

The changes **were caused by** the terrible conditions she witnessed in hospitals during the Crimean War. Many soldiers were dying, not from their wounds, but from illnesses caused by poor hygiene and unclean water.

Historians have described Florence Nightingale as the 'Lady with the Lamp' because of her work caring for wounded soldiers at night.

The power of stories in history

We remember more when things are within a story.

(Professor Daniel Willingham)

Stories have an essential place in the history curriculum. Stories play an important role in developing vocabulary, building rich schemata, and introducing pupils to concepts that they will later explore in the primary years.

The power of stories to support children to access unfamiliar content is also well established. This might include fictional stories that can develop knowledge of concepts (such as 'monarch' or 'government') even when these are not tied to specific historical contexts.

As in later stages, individual stories and rich hinterland (Counsell, 2018) content may establish a more meaningful context for pupils to learn new material, something that Townsend (2019) has explored in Key Stage 1.

Chapter 5: history

Read like an historian

Students without disciplinary awareness may not read such texts with a nuanced understanding or a sufficiently critical eye.

(Shanahan, 2019)

When pupils are reading texts in history, especially at KS2, it is helpful that they learn the subject-specific ways that historians might read a text. In the example below, the generalised reading comprehension strategies, which have an impact of over six months progress according to the EEF, are a good starting point. However, it is then very useful to explore the text through the lens of an historian. This does not mean that all the strategies are used at once but exemplify how we might read a text and articulate our thought process.

Lent et al (2019) advocate the use of a 'I see, I think, I wonder, I connect' graphic organiser to support pupils with their disciplinary reading. It is a more pupil friendly approach to tackling different texts.

This contains the same information as the reading comprehension strategies grid but makes it more accessible for pupils.

I think	I see
'I think that this text is about Sarah Forbes Bonetta (1843–1880). I am thinking that this links to the Victorian times. This is the reason why she became Queen Victoria's goddaughter and why she was historically significant.'	'I can see children in the workhouses during Victorian times.'
I wonder	I connect
'This must be a credible source because it is from Queen Victoria's journals. I wonder how she became her goddaughter. Is her life similar or different to other children in Victorian times?'	'I remember learning about Oliver Twist and the children in the workhouses during Victorian times.'

Generalised Ways	Make predictions	Visualise	Ask questions	Make connections	Clarify	Summarise
History	Think about why a person is significant. Think about the time period.	Think back to the historical period. What can you see and hear?	Think about what is different or similar and what has continued or changed over time. Think about how historians have interpreted an event. E.g. What does this source tell me?	Think about connections between events and draw contrasts.	Are there any historical words that need to be clarified? Who wrote or created this source?	Summarise the key events. Think about trends over time.

What might disciplinary reading look like in practice?

This is to illustrate what a teacher might model to pupils as they are reading historical texts.

Why was Sarah Forbes Bonetta significant in Victorian times?

Sarah Forbes Bonetta (1843–1880) *[Makes predictions. 'I think this text is about Sarah Forbes Bonetta. I am thinking that this links to Victorian times']*, christened with the Yoruba name Aina, was a West African woman who became the goddaughter of Queen Victoria *[Makes predictions. 'I think she might be significant because she was Queen Victoria's adopted goddaughter']*. Her life, documented in sources like Queen Victoria's journals and Captain Forbes's accounts, offers a glimpse into the complexities of race and unexpected connections within the Victorian era *[Asks questions. 'This must be a creditable source because it is from Queen*

Chapter 5: history

Victoria's journals. I wonder how she became her adopted goddaughter? Is her life similar or different to other children in Victorian times?'].

Born around 1843 in what is now southwestern Nigeria *[Asks questions. 'I see that she was from south Nigeria. I wonder how she arrived in England.']*, Aina's early life remains shrouded in some mystery *[Make connections. I remember learning about Oliver Twist and the children in the workhouses during Victorian times.']*. Historical evidence suggests she belonged to the Egbado group of the Yoruba people. During a war with the neighbouring Dahomey kingdom, Aina was captured, likely around the age of five. King Ghezo of Dahomey, a key figure in the transatlantic slave trade, held her captive.

A twist of fate intervened in 1850 when Captain Frederick Forbes, a British Royal Navy officer, arrived in Dahomey on a diplomatic *[Clarify. 'I wonder what that word means?']* mission. They negotiated Aina's release, presenting her as a 'gift' to Queen Victoria. The reasons behind this remain unclear, but historians have focused on causes. Forbes, who had grown fond of Aina, might have seen to it to ensure her safety and future. For Queen Victoria, it could have been a gesture of goodwill towards a potential ally in Africa, or simply a display of British power and 'civilizing' influence.

Upon arriving in England, Aina was rechristened Sarah Forbes Bonetta, symbolically severing ties with her past. Queen Victoria, impressed by her intelligence and dignity, took Sarah under her wing *['This is, perhaps, the reason why she became Queen Victoria's goddaughter and why she was historically significant']*. Sarah received an education, was introduced to British high society, and even developed a close friendship with Queen Victoria's daughter, Princess Alice.

Despite these privileges, Sarah's life was not without its challenges. She existed in a constant negotiation between her African heritage and the expectations of Victorian England. There is evidence of a yearning for her homeland, with Sarah requesting information about her family in Africa on several occasions.

(Text created by Google Gemini)

Talk like an historian

Example 1

Why was Sarah Forbes Bonetta historically significant?

Another reason why she is significant is…

This source tells me that…

Sarah Forbes Bonnetta is significant because…

Example 2: scaffolding responses through concept cartoons

Sarah Forbes Bonnetta is significant because she had a close relationship with Queen Victoria.

Sarah Forbes Bonnetta is significant because she was the first African person to meet Queen Victoria.

Figure 5.5 Concept cartoon

Look at both statements. Do you agree with them? Why or why not? What evidence did you use?

Concept cartoons are a very useful way of promoting discussion and debate. In the second example, there is no sources of evidence to suggest that Sarah *was* the first African to meet Queen Victoria. These are also very useful for reading comprehension answers and supporting all pupils with their discussion and responses.

History talk time: example 3
Sarah Forbes Bonnetta

Sarah Forbes Bonetta (1843–1880), christened with the Yoruba name Aina, was a West African woman who became the goddaughter of Queen Victoria.

This part suggests that she is historically significant.

Teacher questions:

Do you agree or disagree? Why?

What other parts in the text suggest this?

Why do you think that?

Would anyone like to build on this response?

(Incorporating Resnik et al, 2018)

Write like an historian

During the primary years, pupils are exposed to a wide variety of text types that cover a range of audiences and purposes. By the end of primary school, pupils are expected to have a repertoire of grammar and punctuation that they can draw upon. For example, writing and understanding how to use topic sentences to introduce paragraphs or mastering the use of expanded noun phrases. Disciplinary literacy in history requires knowledge of the vocabulary and subject (substantive knowledge) and knowledge of the grammar and syntactical structures. As in English, pupils could be writing a range of text types that can be explored through history.

When writing like an historian in the primary phrase, attention needs to be paid to the age-appropriate expectations of pupils once they reach the end of the primary years. A sound inquiry question at the start of a topic can also become the topic of the disciplinary writing so that pupils can show what they know. The content of the writing should contain some of the following:

- Use historical vocabulary.
- Note connections, draw contrasts and analyse trends over time.
- Change and cause.
- Similarity and difference.

- Historical significance.
- Sources and evidence (including interpretations).

Focus on history writing	Reduced focus on history writing
Using historical vocabulary **Historical significance** Writing about an historically significant person, e.g. Queen Elizabeth II. Exploring their life and why they are important today. **Change and cause** Looking at how things have changed over time and what the cause might be. **Similarity and difference** Exploring how toys today are similar or different to toys in the past. **Sources and evidence** Exploring evidence and discussing how historians have interpreted that evidence.	Writing a diary entry from the point of view of a child during World War II. Writing a diary entry about the experiences of the Great Fire of London. Writing a letter to a child during the Greek times. Writing a wanted poster for Boudicca with a character description. NB: historians may interpret or explore real sources as part of their work, but they are not expected to write a source. For example, Anne Frank's diary is a source that gives us vital information about what life was like as a Jew in WWII. A key question here is, would an historian write a diary as part of their work or are they interpreting the evidence?

There are spaces to write diaries, stories and letters in the English curriculum and to make connections between history and English. For example, drawing on the substantive knowledge in history to write creative recounts of events that have happened in the past. However, it is important that pupils are taught the difference between the two, so that they understand what is distinct and special about writing in history, especially at KS2.

When I first introduced the *Boudicca wanted* posters, many teachers had expressed that this is what they have in their history books. Here are some possible reasons why asking pupils to produce a 'wanted poster' might not be ambitious for the history curriculum.

1. At primary level, historians normally interpret sources, not write them.
2. Wanted posters were not invented when Boudicca was around.
3. It is within the English discipline.
4. For KS2 pupils, is the quality of the writing really what you would expect for older pupils? Or is a simple description more suited to KS1 pupils? We must have high expectations for work produced across the curriculum.

Chapter 5: history

By the end of Key stage 2

History writing text type examples	– Recount an event from the past – Information texts (detailing historical significance) – An account (explaining why an event happened) – Explanation texts (detailing the causes and effects of an event or exploring how historians have interpreted sources and evidence) – Discussion texts (exploring similarities and differences) – Argument/discussion texts (exploring cause and effect or trends)
Features of writing	– Historical vocabulary – Past tense – Active voice – Present tense – Facts and dates – Timelines – Fronted adverbials – Quotes – Formal register – Pictures and diagrams (e.g. sources and evidence)
Disciplinary grammar	**Relative clauses and punctuation for parenthesis** Sarah Forbes Bonetta **(1843–1880), who was christened with the Yoruba name Aina**, was a West African woman who became Queen Victoria's goddaughter. **Subordinate clauses** During a war with the neighbouring Dahomey kingdom, **when she was likely around five years old**, Aina was captured by King Ghezo. **Fronted adverbials (of time)** **Upon arriving in England**, Aina was rechristened Sarah Forbes Bonetta… **In 1850**, when Captain Frederick Forbes, a British Royal Navy officer, arrived in Dahomey on a diplomatic mission. **Past perfect** For Queen Victoria, it could **have been** a gesture of goodwill towards a potential ally in Africa… **Statements** In 1862 **(fronted adverbial)**, Sarah married James Pinson Labulo Davies, a wealthy Sierra Leonean merchant. **Past tense** Sarah received an education, **was introduced** to British high society, and even **developed** a close friendship with Queen Victoria's daughter, Princess Alice **Agentless passive** During a war with the neighbouring Dahomey kingdom, Aina was **captured**, likely around the age of five.

Reading and analysing history writing – upper KS2 example

The Life of Sarah Forbes-Bonnetta

Sarah Forbes Bonetta (1843–1880) *[Introduction. Substantive knowledge: dates and facts]*, christened with the Yoruba name Aina, *[Commas to clarify meaning]* was a West African woman who became the goddaughter of Queen Victoria. Her life, documented in sources like Queen Victoria's journals and Captain Forbes's accounts *[Disciplinary knowledge: drawing on sources and evidence]*, offers a glimpse into the complexities of race and unexpected connections within the Victorian era.

Born around 1843 in what is now southwestern Nigeria *[Fronted adverbials]*, Aina's early life remains shrouded in some mystery. Historical evidence suggests she belonged to the Egbado group of the Yoruba people. During a war with the neighbouring Dahomey kingdom *[Fronted adverbial]*, Aina was captured *[Agentless passive]*, likely around the age of five. King Ghezo of Dahomey, a key figure in the transatlantic slave trade, *[Commas for parenthesis. Ellipsis of the words 'who was…']* held her captive.

A twist of fate intervened in 1850 when Captain Frederick Forbes, a British Royal Navy officer, arrived in Dahomey on a diplomatic mission *[Topic sentence]*. They negotiated Aina's release, presenting her as a 'gift' to Queen Victoria. The reasons behind this remain unclear, but historians have focused on causes *[Disciplinary knowledge: historical cause and consequence]*. Forbes, who had grown fond of Aina, might have seen *[Past perfect]* it as a way to ensure her safety and future. For Queen Victoria, it could have been a gesture of goodwill towards a potential ally in Africa, or simply a display of British power and 'civilizing' *[Historical vocabulary and quotation]* influence.

Upon arriving in England *[Fronted adverbial]*, Aina was rechristened Sarah Forbes Bonetta, symbolically severing ties with her past. Queen Victoria, impressed by her intelligence and dignity, took Sarah under her wing. Sarah received an education, was introduced to British high society, and even developed a close friendship with Queen Victoria's daughter, Princess Alice *[Commas to clarify meaning]*.

Despite these privileges *[Fronted adverbial]*, Sarah's life was not without its challenges. She existed in a constant negotiation between her African heritage and the expectations of Victorian England. There is evidence of a yearning for her homeland, with Sarah requesting information about her family in Africa on several occasions.

Chapter 5: history

In 1862, Sarah married James Pinson Labulo Davies, a wealthy Sierra Leonean merchant *[Topic sentence]*. The couple returned to Africa, settling in Lagos. Sarah continued to correspond with Queen Victoria, but her health declined. She died in Madeira, Portugal, in 1880, at the age of 37 *[Substantive knowledge: key facts and dates]*. Sarah Forbes Bonetta's story compels us to examine the complexities of the British Empire *[Historical significance and the substantive concept of empire]*. Her life, lived between two worlds, offers a unique perspective on race, power and unexpected acts of kindness within a vast and unequal global system *[Disciplinary knowledge: concluding statement and impact of Sarah Forbes Bonetta today (significance)]*.

Sources:

1. Royal Archives, Kew, Victoria's Journals.

2. Forbes, Frederick E. (1851) *Dahomey and the Dahomans: Being a Historical and Ethnographical Account of one of the Least Known Countries of Africa.* Hatchard and Son.

3. National Portrait Gallery. Aina (Sarah Forbes Bonetta (later Davies)). www.npg.org.uk/collections/search/portrait/mw86361/Aina-Sarah-Forbes-Bonetta-later-Davies (Accessed: 04/04/20205)

4. English Heritage. Sarah Forbes Bonetta. www.english-heritage.org.uk/visit/places/osborne/history-and-stories/sarah-forbes-bonetta/ (Accessed: 04/04/20205)

5. Brighton & Hove Museums. 'African princess and Queen Victoria's goddaughter, Sarah Forbes Bonetta (1843–1880). https://www.sussexlive.co.uk/news/history/black-history-month-sarah-forbes-6016935 (Accessed: 04/04/20205)

6. Wikipedia. Sara Forbes Bonetta. https://en.wikipedia.org/wiki/Sara_Forbes_Bonetta (Accessed: 04/04/20205)

(Text created by Google Gemini and edited)

Writing activities

Within English stories (as a subject discipline), pupils are constantly exposed to the structure of Who? What? When? Why? etc. and this structure can easily be used in history writing to support pupils with their information texts. This might be useful for supporting younger (KS1) writers in both English and history.

Who, what, when, why? Structure in history
- **Who?** Sarah Forbes Bonnetta
- **What?** Became the goddaughter of Queen Victoria
- **When?** 1850
- **Why?** Captain Forbes presented her as a gift to Queen Victoria so she could be freed.

Sentence: In 1850, Sarah Forbes Bonetta became the goddaughter of Queen Victoria because her husband (at the time) had offered her as a gift.

Using conjunctions – *because, but, so*
This activity, taken from Hochman and Wexler (2017), requires pupils to think about the disciplinary rigour of their explanations. This is suitable for KS1 pupils who are beginning to explore the use of conjunctions to make their writing more interesting. It not only teaches them the function of conjunctions and how these introduce subordinate clauses, but it also enables them to think critically about the content of their writing and how the conjunction can enable critical analysis and bring depth to their writing. This typically starts with a sentence stem that pupils need to complete. Sentence 3 requires pupils to look at Henry VII with a critical lens. These can then be extended to looking at how a range of conjunctions can support pupils with their historical writing, e.g. *although, while, after, before* etc.

1 **Henry VIII was an excellent king because** he oversaw a period of significant artistic and literary development in England, and supported exploration and shipbuilding which strengthened the English Navy.
2 **Henry VIII was an excellent king, so** England emerged as a more prominent player on the European stage during his reign.
3 **Henry VIII was an excellent king, but** his reign was also marked by religious turmoil due to the English Reformation, extravagant spending that left the treasury depleted, and a reputation for brutality towards those who challenged him.

(Adapted from: Hochman and Wexler 2017)

Case study:
disciplinary literacy in history, an interview with Alex Fairlamb

Alex Fairlamb: Assistant Principal (Teaching and Learning and Secondary Literacy). Secondary Committee member of the Historical Association. Co-editor of *What is History Teaching, Now* and co-author of 'The Scaffolding Effect: Supporting All Students to Succeed'.

School/Academy Trust: Kings Priory School (Reception to Year 13)

Background to the school

This school is a mixed comprehensive in the northeast of England. The school operates across neighbouring sites in the centre of the attractive coastal village of Tynemouth, with short commuting links into Newcastle upon Tyne. The school is close to the ancient Priory, the mouth of the River Tyne and the beach. This historical and picturesque setting provides a stimulating learning opportunity for all pupils.

Kings Priory School is part of Woodard Academies Trust multi-academy sponsor whose aim is to be a provider of world-class education, transforming lives within and across communities.

Books and resources that have supported the school with disciplinary literacy in history

- Bilton, C. and Tillotson, S. (2020) Improving Literacy in KS1: Guidance Report. Education Endowment Foundation. https://d2tic4wvo1iusb.cloudfront.net/production/eef-guidance-reports

/literacy-ks-1/Literacy_KS1_Guidance_Report_2020.pdf?v= 1744623893 (Accessed: 04/04/2025)
- Bilton, C. & Duff, A. (2021) Improving Literacy in KS2: Guidance Report. Education Endowment Foundation. https://d2tic4wvo1iusb.cloudfront.net/production/eef-guidance-reports/literacy-ks2/EEF-Improving-literacy-in-key-stage-2-report-Second-edition.pdf?v=1712494070 (Accessed: 04/04/2025)
- Quigley, A. & Coleman, R. (2021a) Improving Literacy in Secondary Schools: Guidance Report. Education Endowment Foundation. https://educationendowmentfoundation.org.uk/education-evidence/guidance-reports/literacy-ks3-ks4 (Accessed: 04/04/2025)
- Alex Quigley – *Closing the Writing Gap* (2022), *Closing the Reading Gap* (2020) and *Closing the Vocabulary Gap* (2018) all Routledge.
- Christopher Such (2021) – *Art and Science of Teaching Primary Reading*, SAGE. This is also very useful for secondary teachers to read to develop their understanding of reading.
- Katherine Mortimore (2020) – *Disciplinary Literacy and Explicit Vocabulary Teaching: A Whole School Approach to Closing the Attainment Gap*, John Catt.
- Hochmann J.C. and Wexler, N (2017 and 2024) – *The Writing Revolution: A Guide to Advancing Thinking Through Writing in All Subjects and Grades*, Jossey-Bass.

How did you introduce disciplinary literacy and what does it look like now?

The introduction of disciplinary literacy begins in EYFS with books that build schema and lay the foundation for historical knowledge, tying in with the EYFS areas of 'literacy' and 'understanding the world'. Diverse texts are used to illustrate key concepts, particularly in understanding the world. A sequential progression model was created from EYFS to Year 13, ensuring teachers were aware of prior learning and could build upon this meaningfully in an integrated and collaborative way. This is important to ensure learning is continuous and connected, and that the potential danger of a 'transition gap' does not occur within the school.

In Year 1, following learning about history within their living memory, the focus shifted to exploring how people lived in the past, comparing the reigns of Queen Elizabeth I, Queen Victoria and Queen Elizabeth II to understand the concept of monarchy. The Frayer model is utilised throughout the school for explicit vocabulary instruction and so pupils are taught the term 'monarchy' using this graphic organiser. From the start, pupils are encouraged to 'talk like historians' and engage in wider reading, using authentic texts like Floella Benjamin's *Coming to England* to underpin the curriculum.

At primary, teacher-led modelled reading and choral reading is employed to enhance fluency, modelling intonation and expression. The focus is on transforming historical understanding into spoken, written and read forms, emphasising the skills of a historian.

Explicit vocabulary instruction starts in Year 1. This vocabulary is mapped across the school and teachers identify which two to five words will be explicitly taught using the Frayer model, which proves especially beneficial for SEND students.

From Year 3, the approach evolves to include texts like David Olusoga's *Black and British* when studying Roman Britain in Year 4 and Frank Dikotter's *How to be a Dictator* when studying dictatorships in Year 8. Every inquiry is linked to an authentic text, with the time dedicated to reading depending on the age and stage of the students. Younger pupils read more extensively, while older pupils weave texts into their studies throughout the inquiry process. The inquiry question is often derived from the text, and homework may focus on exploring it further.

Reciprocal reading is implemented school wide. Pupils learn to think and read like historians by chunking information, checking vocabulary and applying prior knowledge. They summarise the information to form arguments and to understand and then interrogate the author's interpretation. The principle 'If you can't say it, you can't write it' guides instruction (Talk for Writing Conferences with Pie Corbett & Jamie Thomas). Different types of questions are asked across

KS1–5, which graduate from comprehension to summarisation and then supporting or challenging claims with evidence. From lower KS2 upwards teachers use the *The Writing Revolution* to practise various writing styles and sentence structures.

KS1 assessments are primarily oral, while KS2 writing is gradually elevated over time. Each year, pupils take chronology and substantive knowledge quizzes, and one topic culminates in an extended writing piece. The goal is to develop well-structured paragraphs, prioritising quality over quantity.

Inspirations like Alex Quigley's work and focus on local Black Victorians are incorporated. Christine Counsell's work on storytelling and reading like a historian is woven throughout the curriculum.

How often do you complete a piece of disciplinary writing? How is it organised?

In KS1, assessments are conducted orally, focusing on how pupils utilise their knowledge through spoken language. In KS2, writing is progressively developed over time.

Each year, pupils' complete chronology and substantive knowledge quizzes for every topic. Additionally, one topic per year is chosen for an extended writing piece, allowing them to demonstrate progress over time. For example, a Year 4 essay question could be 'Explain how Britain changed during Roman Rule.' The focus is on building strong paragraphs, emphasising quality over quantity. Steady progress is valued, as exemplified by Donal Hale's work at Trinity Academy.

A balance is struck in teacher workload to allow for consistent reading and writing practice throughout the curriculum. This ensures pupils have ample opportunities to develop their historical literacy skills.

What is your approach to oracy? What are your thoughts on subject specific or disciplinary talk?

In secondary schools, they're in the second year of their literacy and oracy plan, which is gradually integrated throughout the curriculum. They believe in categorising oracy into teaching and learning strategies to promote talk (such as cold calling, turn and talk) and a subject-specific or disciplinary approach to oracy, where it's embedded within each subject area, using strategies like sentence stems.

Kings Priory are deliberately taking a cautious approach, prioritising research and trialling different oracy strategies to ensure effectiveness. Teaching and learning strategies like think-pair-share and cold-calling are implemented school-wide.

Metacognition is another focus, with literacy activities like reading for pleasure alongside disciplinary literacy. They break down disciplinary literacy into its components – reading, writing and speaking like an expert in the subject – to ensure an holistic understanding.

The school empowers subject leaders to take ownership of oracy in their respective domains. The content is paramount, so they encourage teachers to explore and discover the best ways to integrate oracy into their subject-specific teaching.

What advice would you give to schools if they want to implement disciplinary literacy and oracy?

Advice for implementing disciplinary literacy and oracy:

- Provide professional development at multiple levels, including whole-school, departmental, middle leader and individual training.
- Ensure middle leaders receive training before the whole school, enabling them to champion and guide the implementation process.
- Structure professional development in a sequential manner, building on prior knowledge and skills.
- Incorporate disciplinary literacy and oracy training into departmental and phase meetings.
- Encourage the development of oracy within each subject area, such as 'speak like a mathematician'.
- Collaborate with experts in fields like music, art and design and technology to enhance disciplinary literacy and oracy practices.
- Adopt a formative approach to professional development, focusing on continuous improvement and feedback.
- Foster a culture of psychological safety, where teachers feel comfortable experimenting and learning from their experiences.

- Implement changes gradually, pausing to assess and consolidate knowledge before moving forward.

Are there any misconceptions in primary schools that as a secondary trained teacher, you would like us to know?

A common misconception in primary schools regarding oracy is the belief that it simply means having pupils talk. However, effective oracy involves scaffolded and purposeful talk, not just any talk activity.

Attempting to strictly evidence every instance of oral communication can lead to a detrimental focus on documentation rather than meaningful learning. Instead, it's crucial to observe learning walks and engage in conversations with pupils to assess their oracy skills and understanding.

The role of disciplinary literacy and oracy is key. Pupils need to use the language and discourse of an historian in the making, and so time should be given to subject leads and teachers to explore what this means within their lessons. Reading, writing and speaking like an historian is different to how a scientist, geographer or linguist reads, writes and speaks. We should celebrate, elevate and emphasise these differences, ensuring that pupils recognise these nuances and differences too.

References and bibliography

Counsell, C. (2018). Blog. Senior Curriculum Leadership 1: The indirect manifestation of knowledge: (A) curriculum as narrative. https://thedignityofthethingblog.wordpress.com/2018/04/07/senior-curriculum-leadership-1-the-indirect-manifestation-of-knowledge-a-curriculum-as-narrative/ (Accessed: 04/04/25)

DfE (2014). History Programmes of Study: KS1 and KS2. https://assets.publishing.service.gov.uk/media/5a7c2917e5274a1f5cc762cf/PRIMARY_national_curriculum_-_History.pdf (Accessed: 04/04/20205)

Harris, R. (2021) Disciplinary knowledge denied? In: Chapman, A. (ed.) *Knowing History in Schools: Powerful Knowledge and the Powers of Knowledge. Knowledge and the curriculum.* UCL Press, 97–128.

Case study: disciplinary literacy in history, an interview with Alex Fairlamb

Hochman, J & Wexler, N. (2017) *The Writing Revolution*. Jossey-Bass.

Lawton, D. (1988) The National Curriculum since 1988: panacea or poisoned chalice? *Forum*, 50(3), pp.337–342.

Lent, R. C. & Voigt, M. M. (2018) *Disciplinary Literacy in Action: How to Create and Sustain a School-Wide Culture of Deep Reading, Writing, and Thinking*. SAGE Publications.

Ofsted (2021) Research review series: https://www.gov.uk/government/publications/research-review-series-history/research-review-series-history (Accessed: 04/04/20205)

Ofsted (2023) History subject review: rich encounters with the past. https://www.gov.uk/government/publications/subject-report-series-history/rich-encounters-with-the-past-history-subject-report (Accessed: 04/04/20205)

Shanahan, T. (2019) Disciplinary Literacy in Primary Schools. https://ncca.ie/media/4679/disciplinary-literacy-in-the-primary-school-professor-timothy-shanahan-university-of-illinois-at-chicago-1.pdf (Accessed: 04/04/20205)

Spires, H., Kerkhoff, S. N. & Paul, C. M. (n.d.) (2020) *Read, Write, Inquire: Disciplinary Literacy in Grades 6-12*. Teachers College Press.

Townsend, S. (2019) Up Pompeii: studying a significant event at key stage 1. *Primary History*, 82, 18–23.

Wineburg, S., Martin, D. & Monte-Sano, C. (2011) *Reading Like a Historian*. Teachers College Press.

Further reading and subject knowledge

Tiffany, S. (2023) *Mr T Does Primary History*. Corwin Press.

Fairlamb, A. & Ball, R. (2023) *What is History Teaching, Now? A Practical Handbook for All History Teachers and Educators*. Hodder Education.

Chapter 6:
science

Scientists, unlike historians, do not have to wait for an event to have occurred prior to undertaking an investigation. With experiments, they can control circumstances in ways that allow them to focus on a particular variable of interest.

(Shanahan, 2019)

While scientific writing will contain both substantive and disciplinary knowledge, it is useful to unpick the difference between the two to understand what pupils need to know to write successfully as a scientist. As mentioned earlier, both aspects are essential as pupils need to have the substantive knowledge to write detailed explanation and information texts by the time they complete their primary school years. From experience, most pupils automatically write within the science discipline. This was the subject that took me the least amount of time to implement, as many aspects were already in place in books. The focus was on providing opportunities to write at length and to be deliberate and considered about the kind of knowledge that we want pupils to demonstrate in their writing (this could also be oral).

Substantive knowledge (facts)	Disciplinary knowledge (how scientists acquire the substantive knowledge)
For example: identify and name wild and garden plants; light and shadows; forces and magnets; solids, liquids and gases; evaporation and condensation; the theory of evolution and the solar system.	For example, scientific skills include: asking questions; observing closely; using equipment; performing tests; identifying; classifying; gathering and recording data.

Speaking and thinking like a scientist – language frames for scientific experiments

These language stems were written based on the 'working scientifically' aspect of the national curriculum. They do not cover all aspects but focus on the scientific experiments that pupils are most likely to write.

Nursery and Reception (Prompts for adults)	I have used this scientific equipment because... This is a fair test because... These diagrams, labels and tables etc show that... I think this because... The results show that... I think this means...
KS1	I have used this scientific equipment because... This is a fair test because... These diagrams, labels and tables etc. show that... I think this because... The results show that... I have concluded that... My explanation is...The relationship is...
KS2	I have used this scientific equipment because... This is a fair test because...I predict that... The results show that/are reliable because... I have concluded that... My explanation is...The relationship is...

EYFS

Examples	Adult modelling and questioning
I have used this scientific equipment because...	'We are going to use a magnifying glass as part of our **scientific equipment**...'
The results show that...	'**The results show that** this boat floated but this rock is sinking.'
This is a fair test because...	'**This is a fair test because** we have used the same magnet each time.'

Chapter 6: science

KS1 and KS2

In KS1, pupils will be beginning to write up their explanations of what they have learned so that they can show what they know and understand about a particular concept. Like history, this could be one sentence in Year 1, before building up to a paragraph in Year 2. In quite a few schools, longer pieces of writing were only dedicated to Year 2 onwards, with simple sentences in Year 1. As previously mentioned, disciplinary writing is about quality and not quantity.

Read like a scientist

	Generalised ways	Make predictions	Visualise	Ask questions	Make connections	Clarify	Summarise
Science		Make a hypothesis about what is going to happen. Think about the subject matter.	Use diagrams and pictures to understand key processes.	Discuss the key concepts and why they are happening. E.g. *What helps the plant to grow? How did you ...?', 'Why does this ...?',* and *'What makes me think that ...?', 'What do you mean by that ...?'* (EEF, 2023)	Connect with previous science topics or other curriculum areas, e.g. mathematics.	Think about the key vocabulary and discuss their meanings.	In explanation texts, summarise five key scientific aspects, e.g. the plant life cycle or what materials conduct electricity.

Science writing

This exemplifies what a teacher might 'think aloud', when they are reading a scientific text.

121

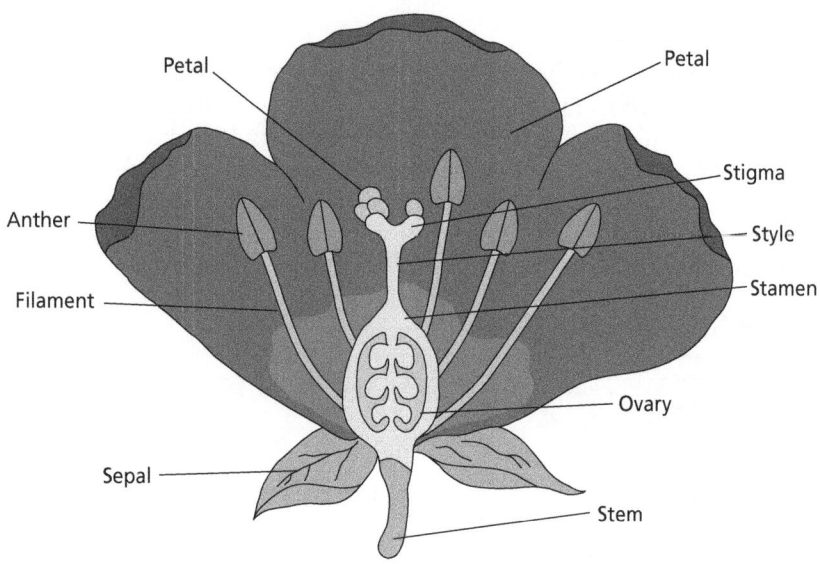

Figure 6.1 Parts of a flower

Flowering plants *[Make predictions. I think that this text is going to be about flowering plants]*. I remember learning about flowers when I was younger and growing our own cress. Plants, like many living things, have a special cycle of life. This cycle has different stages, each one important for the plant to live and make more of its kind. It's controlled by things inside the plant, like its genes, and things outside, like the weather.

The first stage starts with a seed. Inside this tiny package is a baby plant, food to help it grow and a protective coat. The seed can stay asleep for a long time, even years, until the right conditions come along. When it's warm and wet enough, the seed wakes up and starts to sprout *[Ask questions. I have observed that the temperature and the water support seeds to grow. I wonder what would be a long time to wait?]*. A tiny root pushes out first, helping the seedling hold on tight in the soil. Then, a shoot grows upwards, reaching for the sunlight. The first leaves, called cotyledons, appear and start making food for the growing plant.

The seedling grows quickly *[Make connections. I think this links to making observations when we carry out science experiments and mathematics, when we count how long it takes to grow]*, its roots digging deeper into the soil to find water and nutrients. The shoot stretches taller and new leaves appear. These leaves use sunlight, air and water to make food through a process called photosynthesis.

After this initial growth spurt, the plant enters a longer stage where it keeps getting bigger. Its stem grows taller, more leaves sprout, and it might even start making buds, which will eventually turn into flowers.

The flowering stage is all about making new seeds. The buds open up into colourful flowers with male and female parts. The male part makes pollen, which can be carried by the wind or insects to the female part of another flower. If this happens, the flower is pollinated *[Clarify meaning. I wonder what this means?]* and a seed starts to grow inside.

The seed is protected inside a fruit, which might be brightly coloured or smell good to attract animals. These animals eat the fruit and then spread the seeds in their droppings, helping new plants grow in different places.

And so, the cycle begins again with a new seed, ready to sprout and grow into a beautiful flowering plant. Understanding this cycle helps us appreciate how amazing plants are and how they fit into the world around us. *[Summarise. 1. The cycle begins with a seed; 2. When warmth and moisture are sufficient, the seed grows; 3. The seedling experiences rapid growth, with roots expanding for nutrient and water uptake; 4. The plant matures, producing buds that bloom into flowers with male and female parts; 5. Seeds develop within fruits, often attractive to animals to eat and the cycle starts again.]*

(Created by Google Gemini and edited.)

In all of the sciences, argumentation is one of the central means through which practitioners test new ideas and theories.

(Resnik et al, 2018)

Science talk time

Example 1

Concept cartoons are a great way to build in structured talk time and to address and discuss any misconceptions.

Figure 6.2 Concept cartoon

'Look at the statements. Do you agree with them? Why or why not? What makes you think that?'

Concept cartoons are a very useful way of promoting discussion and debate. In the first statement, discussion can focus on plants that do not produce flowers, like moss. The second and third statements might address the role of roots and stems in transporting nutrients and water.

Teacher questions:

Do you agree or disagree? Why?

What other parts in the text suggest this?

Why do you think that?

Would anyone like to build on this response?

(Incorporating Resnik et al., 2018)

Example 2

Why are animals important within the life cycle of a plant?

They are important because…

Write like a scientist

Scientists write in unique and specialised ways that differ from history or geography writing. We can draw on our knowledge from English, e.g. using paragraphing and varying the use of expanded noun phrases. Science writing tends to focus heavily on expanded noun phrases, 'approximately 60% of words in science texts are nouns' (Biber and Gray, 2017, taken from Shanahan, 2019). The writing tends to be more formal, with abstract nouns and more subject specific vocabulary. From experience, most pupils tend to write in scientific ways and teachers have reported that they do this automatically. Therefore, this chapter will break scientific writing down further and focus on what it could look like.

Focus on science writing	Reduced focus on science writing
– Write up of a science experiment with a hypothesis and conclusion – Procedural account – Explanation texts, e.g. how materials conduct electricity – Information texts, e.g. on animals or plant life etc.	– A diary from the point of view of an animal – A letter to a local zoo thanking them for your recent visit NB: all of these examples are perfect for English lessons, where pupils can draw on their science knowledge in English. This does not mean that they never write like this. In their work, would scientists write a creative story or diary?

As with history writing, there is space to write diaries, stories and letters in the English curriculum and to make connections between science and English.

By the end of Key Stage 2, pupils should be familiar with these features of writing and grammar:

Science writing text type examples	Features of science writing
– Experiments – Procedural recounts – Explanations – Arguments – Information texts	– Scientific vocabulary – Nouns and noun phrases – Precise verbs and modal verbs – Precision – Abstract nouns – Formal tone – Subordinate clause – Passive voice and agentless passive – Standard English – Prepositional phrases – Pictures and diagrams

Disciplinary grammar	**Expanded noun phrases** *Flowering plants undergo a **well-defined life cycle**...* *These changes can be anything from **a slightly thicker beak** in a bird...* **Modal verbs** *Sometimes, these genes **can** (modal verb) get copied incorrectly, which creates a **mutation** (abstract noun).* **Abstract nouns** ***Evolution** (abstract noun) explains how living things change over time.* **Passive voice** *These changes **are caused by** (passive voice) something called **genes** (abstract noun), which are like tiny instruction manuals that tell an animal how to build its body.* **Prepositional phrases** *...birds migrate **in the direction of**...* ***In the past**...* **Adverbs** *This **gradually** changed...* *The number of birds has **significantly** declined.* **Subordinate clauses** *The stamen produces pollen grains, **which** can be dispersed by wind or pollinators to the carpel's stigma.* **Fronted adverbials** ***Following fertilisation**, the carpel develops into a fruit, containing seeds that hold the potential for a new generation of plants.*

Chapter 6: science

The table outlines the features of grammar that might be more prevalent in science writing at the primary stage. Some teachers make this explicit for pupils and others only teach this explicitly in the English sessions. The focus should be on displaying pupils' substantive and disciplinary knowledge.

Science writing

Flowering plants, like many living things, have a special cycle of life *[Substantive knowledge: explaining the life cycle]*. This cycle has different stages, each one important for the plant to live and make more of its kind. It is controlled by things inside the plant and things outside, like the weather *[Formal language: no contractions or similes/metaphors etc.]*.

The first stage starts with a seed. Inside this tiny package *[Expanded noun phrases]* is a baby plant, food to help it grow and a protective coat. The seed can stay asleep for a long time, even years, until the right conditions come along. When it is warm and wet enough *[Tier 3 vocabulary and substantive knowledge]*, the seed wakes up and starts to sprout *[Substantive knowledge: what seeds need to grow]*. A tiny root pushes out first, helping the seedling hold on tight in the soil. Then, a shoot grows upwards, reaching for the sunlight. The first leaves appear and start making food for the growing plant.

The seedling grows quickly, its roots digging deeper into the soil to find water and nutrients *[Tier 3 vocabulary]*. The shoot stretches taller and new leaves appear. These leaves use sunlight, air and water to make food through a process called photosynthesis.

After this initial growth spurt, the plant enters a longer stage where it keeps getting bigger. Its stem grows taller, more leaves sprout, and it might even start making buds, which will eventually turn into flowers.

The flowering stage is all about making new seeds. The buds open into colourful flowers with male and female parts. The male part makes pollen, which can be carried by the wind or insects to the female part of another flower. If this happens, the flower is pollinated *[Tier 3 vocabulary]* and a seed starts to grow inside.

The seed is protected inside a fruit, which might be brightly coloured or smell good to attract animals. These animals eat the fruit and then spread the seeds in their droppings, helping new plants grow in different places *[Substantive knowledge]*.

And so, the cycle begins again with a new seed, ready to sprout and grow into a beautiful flowering plant. Understanding this cycle helps us appreciate how amazing plants are and how they fit into the world around us.

(Text created by Google Gemini)

References

Castek, J., & Beach, R. (2013) Using apps to support disciplinary literacy and science learning. *Journal of Adolescent & Adult Literacy*, 56(7), 554–564.

Education Endowment Foundation (2023). Improving Primary Science: Guidance Report. https://d2tic4wvo1iusb.cloudfront.net/production/eef-guidance-reports/primary-science-ks1-ks2/improving-primary-science-guidance-report-ks1-ks2.pdf?v=1723581620 (Accessed 04/04/2025)

Hochman, J. & Wexler, N. (2017) *The Writing Revolution*. Jossey-Bass.

Haland, A. (2016) Disciplinary literacy in elementary school: how a struggling student positions herself as a writer. *The Reading Teacher*, 70(4), 457–468.

Shanahan, T. (2019) Disciplinary Literacy in Primary Schools. https://ncca.ie/media/4679/disciplinary-literacy-in-the-primary-school-professor-timothy-shanahan-university-of-illinois-at-chicago-1.pdf (Accessed 04/04/2025)

Further reading

Rogers, B. Primary science – How and why Paradigm Trust overhauled its science curriculum. www.teachwire.net/news/primary-science-how-and-why-paradigm-trust-overhauled-its-science-curriculum/ (Accessed: 04/04/2025)

Chapter 7: geography

Disciplinary knowledge (the knowledge of how geographical knowledge is formed, debated and contested) was a weaker area of curriculum thinking in both primary and secondary schools.

(Ofsted, 2023)

Geography is an interdisciplinary subject that draws on not only science, history and mathematics, but the specific skills of a geographer. Their thinking and speaking skills are clearly very distinct. Johnson et al (2011) simplify the study of geography as having, 'two main practices: human geography and physical geography.' However, they stress that both are connected to each other and are not disparate.

The phrase to 'think like a geographer' has long been used. It captures how pupils can learn to:

- Use what they know from one context in another.
- Think about alternative futures.
- Consider their influence on decisions that will be made.

This draws on the concept of interconnection. It manifests itself through pupils asking questions such as, *'Where is this place?', 'Why is it here and not there?', 'What is it like?', 'How did it get like this?'* and *'What would it feel like to live in this place?'*

(Source: Ofsted research reviews: geography, 2021 and Storm, 1988)

If we can establish that very young pupils are enabled to make these inquiry questions, then this will support them with rich discussions later in their primary years.

Speaking and thinking like a geographer – language frames

These sentence stems were written based on the national curriculum and the disciplinary knowledge that is particular to geography.

Nursery and Reception (Prompts for adults)	This place is like… This place is changing because… In the future… This is the same as…
KS1	This place is like this because… This place is changing because… This environment is a… (e.g. city, coastal town etc) because… This is similar/different because… I can locate…on a map, globe, or atlas… This is connected because…
KS2	To conclude, the facts I have gathered tell me that… From undertaking fieldwork, I have observed that… This place is affected by human activity because… This physical/human characteristic is similar/different because… From analysing…I've concluded that…

EYFS

Development matters – understanding the world. EYFS pupils should be equipped to:

- Explore the natural world around them.
- Describe what they see, hear and feel while outside.
- Recognise some environments that are different from the one in which they live.
- Understand the effect of changing seasons on the natural world around them.
- Recognise some similarities and differences between life in this country and life in other countries.
- Draw information from a simple map.

- Recognise some similarities and differences between life in this country and life in other countries.

As with history and science, other areas of learning can also support young pupils with their geographical knowledge. For example, reading stories that explore maps or location can also help pupils to build rich schemata.

Examples	Adult modelling and questioning
This place is like…	'This country can be hot and cold, but it is **different** in Trinidad because it is hot all year round.' '**This place is** hot because of where it is in the world.'
This place is changing because…	'**This place is changing because** there are lots more cars.'
In the future…	'**In the future**, there might not be so many trees because people are cutting them down.' [Whilst playing outside]
This is the same as…	'The weather in **Newcastle is the same as** London.'

Read like a geographer

Geographers read differently to mathematicians or scientists, especially when reading and decoding maps. Although the sections of the reading comprehension strategies can also be used in geography, as shown in the table below, schools can also focus on graphicacy. Graphicacy, as opposed to literacy or numeracy, is the special ways that geographers read and decode maps. It is the way in which we read photographs, diagrams and maps, especially symbols and keys, and how we use them (Mackintosh, 2011 and Barlow et al, 2019).

Graphicacy is the ability to understand and present information in the form of graphic images – this includes maps. Every time a geographer uses a map, they are thinking spatially.

(Geographical Association)

Generalised ways	Make predictions	Visualise	Ask questions	Make connections	Clarify	Summarise
Geography	Think about geography lessons in previous years to predict what might happen next.	Use maps, diagrams, globes and aerial photographs to understand geographical concepts.	Where relevant: 'Why is this place like this?', 'How is this place changing?' and 'How are other places affected?' (Ofsted, 2021).	Make connections with other subjects, e.g. science and mathematics.	Is there any geographical vocabulary that needs to be discussed and clarified?	Summarise the three things you have learnt.

Write like a geographer

What is geography writing?	What is not geography writing?
– Writing a map (with a key) of the local area (Year 1 example). – Writing about how rivers, people and land affect each other. – Writing about the impact of climate change on the global population. – Fieldwork report. – Writing about changes to the landscape/environment etc. – Writing about the human and physical features of the local area (Year 2 example).	– A piece of persuasive writing objecting to a planning application. – A letter to the council complaining about the rubbish outside the school. – A poem on the importance of looking after the environment. NB: all of these examples are perfect for English lessons, where pupils can draw on their geographical knowledge in English. This does not mean that they never write like this. In their work, would geographers write a creative story or diary?

Chapter 7: geography

By the end of Key Stage 2, pupils should be familiar with the following geography writing skills:

Geography writing examples	– Discussions – Explanations – Arguments – Information texts – Reports – Descriptive text – Labelled maps
Features of writing	– Standard English – Formal tone – Facts – Statistics – Prepositions – Past, present and future tense – Fronted adverbials – Passive voice – Pictures and diagrams – Subordinating conjunctions (*if*, *when*)
Disciplinary grammar	**Abstract nouns** *Climate change (abstract noun)*, *like a giant wave, is making big changes to this map.* Abstract nouns: *climate change* (abstract noun), *food shortage* (abstract noun), *sea level rise* (abstract noun), *renewable energy* (abstract noun). **Facts** *Scientists believe the average global temperature has already increased by* **1 degree Celsius (fact)** *since the late 19th century…* **Statistics** *Did you know that in some parts of Africa, rainfall has decreased by* **20% (statistic)** *in recent decades?* **Preposition** *We can also plant more trees, which help to soak up* **(preposition)** *the greenhouse gases in* **(preposition)** *the air.* **Fronted adverbials** ***By working together****, we can create a healthier planet for everyone…* **Subordinating conjunctions and modal verbs** ***If*** *extreme weather events become more common, millions of people* ***could*** *be affected by food shortages.*

Geography writing example

How does climate change impact on our world? (with annotations)

Imagine a giant map with all the countries of the world. Climate change, like a giant wave, is making big changes to this map.

Our planet Earth is warming up because of special gases in the air, called greenhouse gases *[Subject specific vocabulary]*. These gases come from things like burning coal and oil for energy. Scientists believe the average global temperature has already increased by one degree Celsius *[Substantive knowledge: key facts]* since the late 19th century, and it is getting warmer even faster now. As Earth warms, the weather is getting more extreme. Some places are getting much hotter and drier *[Disciplinary knowledge: change and the future]*, experiencing droughts that can last for months. Did you know that in some parts of Africa, rainfall has decreased by 20% *[statistic]* in recent decades? While other areas are getting more floods and storms.

These changes are going to make it harder for people to grow food in some areas *[Disciplinary knowledge: impact of climate change]*. Imagine a big field of wheat – if it does not rain enough, the wheat will not grow and people will not have enough food to eat. This is called food shortage. If *[Subordinating conjunction]* extreme weather events become more common, millions of people could be affected by food shortages.

The oceans around the world are also rising. This is because the ice at the top and bottom of the Earth (like giant snowmen!) is melting *[Geographical substantive knowledge]*. As the water melts, it fills up the oceans, making the sea level rise. Scientists predict that sea levels could rise by up to a metre by the end of this century, threatening coastal cities and towns around the world *[Substantive knowledge: facts]*.

Just like some insects spread diseases, climate change can also make some illnesses more common. Warmer weather can help these insects spread and make people sick.

The good news is that we can still work together to tackle climate change! We can use cleaner types of energy, like sunshine and wind, to power our homes and schools. We can also plant more trees, which help to soak up the greenhouse gases in the air.

By working together, we can create a healthier planet for everyone, with less extreme weather, enough food to grow and safe places to live.

(Text created by Google Gemini)

References and bibliography

Barlow, A. & Whitehouse, S. (2019) *Mastering Primary Geography*. Bloomsbury.

Johnson, H., Watson, P. A., Delahunty, T., McSwiggen, P. & Smith, T. (2011) What it is they do: differentiating knowledge and literacy practices across content disciplines. *Journal of Adolescent & Adult Literacy*, 55(2), 100–109.

Mackintosh, M. (2011) Graphicacy for life. *Primary Geography*, 75, 6–7.

Ofsted (2021) Ofsted research reviews: geography. www.gov.uk/government/publications/research-review-series-geography/research-review-series-geography (Accessed 04/04/2025)

Ofsted (2023) Research and analysis. Getting our bearings: geography subject report. www.gov.uk/government/publications/subject-report-series-geography/getting-our-bearings-geography-subject-report (Accessed 04/04/2025)

Shanahan, T. (2019) Disciplinary Literacy in Primary Schools. https://ncca.ie/media/4679/disciplinary-literacy-in-the-primary-school-professor-timothy-shanahan-university-of-illinois-at-chicago-1.pdf (Accessed 04/04/2025)

Storm, M. (1998) The five basic questions for primary geographer. *Primary Geography*, 2, 4–5.

Chapter 8
case study example:
Knowledge Schools Trust, disciplinary literacy – science, history and geography, an interview with Juli Ryzop

Author comment: I am incredibly grateful to the Knowledge Schools Trust who generously shared their innovative and forward-thinking work on disciplinary literacy in primary schools. They are leading in this field of disciplinary literacy.

Academy Trust: Knowledge Schools Trust

Juli Ryzop works for the Knowledge Schools Trust. Previously, she was the Senior Curriculum Advisor for the Primary Knowledge Curriculum (PKC). Juli now works as the Deputy Headteacher across West London Free School Primary and Earl's Court Free School Primary and continues to work in the trust's central school improvement team, offering advice, support, challenge and professional development to the seven primaries within the trust. Juli has a keen interest in the development of disciplinary literacy at primary.

Background to the trust

The Knowledge Schools Trust (KST) is a multi-academy trust with seven primary schools and two secondary schools across London, Buckinghamshire, and Bedfordshire. The trust is known for developing the Primary Knowledge Curriculum (PKC), a knowledge-rich curriculum that places "powerful knowledge" at the heart of learning. Through a deep respect of the traditions of each unique subject, the PKC recognises the identity of the disciplines that are studied. The vision and intent were to create a specified, well-sequenced, and ambitious curriculum for all pupils . The PKC has an impressive 400 partner schools that use their resources.

Was there any research that you used to support you?

- E.D Hirsch: Role of background knowledge.
- Michael Young: Powerful knowledge.
- Timothy Shanahan: Disciplinary literacy.
- Seigfried Englemann: Direct Instruction. I do, we do, you do
- Barak Rosenshine: Principles of instruction.
- Lauren Resnick: Accountable talk – reasoning and providing justification for answers.

Educationalists:

- Doug Lemov: Habits of discussion.
- Claire Sealy: Talking floats on a sea of write.
- Alex Quigley: *Closing the Vocabulary/Reading/Writing Gap.*

How did you introduce disciplinary literacy and what does it look like now?

In 2020, we asked staff to upload one or two examples of pupils' work from each of our history, geography and science units per half-term. What this did was allow us to analyse pupil outcomes across our primaries. We noticed from the outcomes, and further book looks, pupil voice and learning walks on the ground, that our pupils' substantive knowledge was very strong. They could recall key ideas, places, events and people from across our foundation subjects. However, it was also apparent that our pupils' disciplinary knowledge and understanding, and thereby the ability to translate this into their written outcomes, was not as secure. What we were seeing in the pupils' outcomes was that they were predominately writing to entertain (e.g. *'Let me tell you about these awesome and amazing ancient Egyptians. Read on to find out more...'*) instead of writing to communicate effectively in a way that would be unique to the subject discipline. Although the substantive knowledge was accurate, their writing was informal, often switching from first person to third, and incorporated creative writing techniques, such as figurative language or expanded noun phrases, which were not appropriate at times to the subject sensitivity they were writing about.

After digging into this further, we identified two key issues. Firstly, as a central curriculum team we needed to audit the tasks we had specified on the lesson plans to ensure that they were purposefully designed to get the pupils thinking about both the substantive and disciplinary knowledge associated with the subject. Some of the written tasks our staff uploaded incorporated examples of diary entries, letters, posters and leaflets – all layouts that distracted our pupils, especially our older pupils, from communicating academically. Secondly, we wanted to work on enhancing our own teachers' and leaders' subject knowledge regarding the disciplinary aspects of the subjects they were teaching, so that during their own delivery or resource-making, they understood where the disciplinary knowledge was incorporated and thereby were making carefully considered decisions that reflected the nuance of the subject discipline.

Later in 2021, we at PKC updated our history, science and geography unit rationale documents to clarify to our teachers the disciplinary concepts that were being emphasised within our lesson plans. For context, every unit has what we call a unit rationale; this is a document that highlights the purpose of that exact unit being placed in that exact place within our curriculum. The unit rationales explain what has come before and what comes after. They highlight the key end goals of each unit and highlight the key substantive concepts (e.g. empire, trade, migration) that are being built upon in that unit, as well as what the key disciplinary strands are (e.g. causation for history or observing over time for science, etc.).

Following this, we designed and led a series of CPD sessions for our staff on understanding the nuance of disciplinary knowledge for each subject, and later I wrote a series of training sessions on how to effectively write as an historian, geographer, or scientist. This training got teachers to carefully understand and consider how professionals in their respective fields of history, geography and science think, speak, read and write. For example, it was important to us that our teachers understood that history is a story that historians tell about the past, but that the past can be contested and it can change over time. We wanted them to understand the framework in which historians work when researching the past and understanding the meaning of causation, consequence, similarities and differences, continuity and change, and the purpose of sources, evidence and historical interpretation when studying the past. It was essential to start with getting teachers to truly understand the disciplinary knowledge associated with each subject before delving into the nuance of disciplinary literacy.

Our teachers then began to use, during their delivery, simple phrases such as *'Some historians argue...others believe that...'* or *'Evidence from...suggests that...'* or *'Scientists have observed that...'* which brought to the surface for the pupils either the degree of certainty or uncertainty regarding what they were being taught. As Christine Counsell (2018) summarises, we wanted our teachers, and thereby our pupils, to understand that disciplinary knowledge is the 'knowledge that continues to be revised by scholars or professional practice.'

For us, we wanted our staff to understand that disciplinary literacy refers to the specific ways of reading, writing, speaking and thinking that are characteristic of different academic disciplines, and that each discipline has its unique language, practices and ways of constructing knowledge. Building on this point, we wanted our staff to understand that disciplinary writing involves marrying together substantive, disciplinary and procedural knowledge.

We then began to delve down into the depth of each subject discipline and began to unpick the nuances between the three subjects in terms of their disciplinary grammar. Disciplinary grammar refers to

Case study example: Knowledge School Trust, disciplinary literacy

the specific grammatical structures and conventions used within a particular discipline. It concerns understanding how language is used to construct meaning and communicate ideas within that discipline. Disciplinary grammar encompasses the vocabulary, sentence structures and stylistic choices that are characteristic of a particular field of study.

 Historian	⚛ Scientist	Geography
Grammar & Language	**Grammar & Language**	**Grammar & Language**
• Academic	• Academic	• Academic
• Formal	• Formal	• Formal
• Subject-specific	• Subject-specific	• Subject-specific
• Past tense	• Technical & Precise	• Statistical & quantitative
• Past perfect (e.g had been)	• Modal verbs	• Interdisciplinary shifts
• Active voice (more often)	• Passive voice (more often)	• Past tense
• Neutral (no intensifiers)	• Past tense	• Present tense
• Fronted adverbials of time	• Present tense	• Future tense (e.g. will/shall)
• Subordinate clauses (contextual information)	• Future tense (e.g. will/shall)	• Fronted adverbials of place
	• Active voice (more often)	• Prepositions
	• Fronted adverbials of sequence	

Figure 8.1 Disciplinary grammar

We wanted our staff to understand the similarities and differences between the three subjects and the expectations we may be implicitly placing on our pupils when asking them to write like a historian, scientist or geographer. We wanted our teachers to understand that passive voice is often used in science. This is because science is the story of the materials, and the agent of the action (e.g. the scientist) tends to be omitted from the research write ups (e.g. *'The cells were extracted by ultrasonication'*). In contrast, with historical writing, the importance of using the active voice when the agent of the action needs to be given ownership is emphasised (e.g. *'The Nazis deported 440,000 Jews from Hungary'*). Having this written in the passive voice would read as *'440,000 Jews were deported by the Nazis'*, which can conceal agency and signals an unwillingness to state what was really going on.

All resources, readings and materials exposed to the pupils are now written in a style that reflects the historian, scientist or geographer's voice so that both they and the teachers have a clear, secure model to follow. Staff receive continuous professional development (CPD) throughout the year, and curriculum slides are checked by experts to ensure accuracy and effectiveness as part of our monitoring cycle, and feedback is given to staff so that they can develop more expertise and effectiveness when designing resources.

How often do you complete a piece of disciplinary writing? How is it organised?

Every history, geography or science lesson is an opportunity for pupils to engage in disciplinary writing, whether that is in their exercise books or on mini whiteboards. Our teachers are skilled at giving in-the-moment feedback to their pupils so that any misconceptions can immediately be addressed (e.g. using contractions instead of uncontracted forms). For us, we have written tasks that predominately get pupils explaining, describing, recounting, discussing or comparing, depending on the subject.

Table 8.1 Disciplinary text types

History			
Narrative Recount	Descriptive	Analytical	Argumentative
Science			
Explanatory	Descriptive	Argumentative	Discussion
Geography			
Explanatory	Descriptive	Comparative	Statistical Interpretation

In addition to the pupils' weekly foundation subject lessons, in KS2 we have also given five lessons of English curriculum time each half-term over to teaching explicitly how to write like an historian, geographer or scientist. During these lessons we teach the grammar and language that is unique to each discipline. The focus is on enhancing English language skills while utilising the background knowledge gained from the foundation subjects. For example, when discussing prepositions with Year 3s, we emphasise their importance in geography because they help describe the spatial relationships and locations of places, features and phenomena on Earth. We explain that geographers need to use precise language when describing how objects, places and environments are situated relative to each other (e.g. *'Bath is situated in the Southwest of England, located just east of Bristol'*). Although we use English curriculum time for these lessons, our pupils write up their final pieces of work in their history, geography and science books so that they have strong models to refer to during their next unit. The goal is to ensure the pupils's non-fiction writing is as strong as their fiction. These English lessons link to the national curriculum grammar requirements that are outlined for each year group (e.g. Year 3s focus on prepositions and observe how these relate to geography; Year 4s focus on fronted adverbials of time and observe how these could be used by historians; Year 5s focus on modal verbs and observe how these are essential for scientists when describing certainty or possibility and so on).

Pupils with SEND receive additional support through writing frames and scaffolds, with an emphasis on visuals and content being broken down into small, manageable chunks. For our pupils with SEND, or those with writing barriers, the primary focus during our foundation subject lessons is on understanding the knowledge goals, rather than worrying about perfect transcription. Whereas, during English lessons, grammar and punctuation feedback is given.

In terms of organising a piece of disciplinary writing, this will be dependent on the purpose of the writing. If the purpose is to answer an essay question (e.g. *'What motivated Britain to build an empire?'*), then we would explicitly teach the pupils to structure their writing into an opening that references the essay question that they will be answering, the main body of the essay which may recount events and presents evidence, interpretations and arguments, and then the closing which summarises the essay. If the purpose is to write up a scientific experiment, then we would explicitly teach the pupils to organise their writing in accordance with this, such as including an introduction, a list of equipment, the methodology, the results, a discussion and the conclusion. As this incorporates several features, for our young pupils in Year 3, we may break this down over the year so that in one unit, we focus specifically on introduction writing, and then in the following unit, we may solely focus on writing a secure methodology and so on. It is not until the summer term of Year 5 that we ask pupils to pull all this together and when we do, this is heavily scaffolded to begin with. In our trust, every teacher has a visualiser in their classroom and they would use this to facilitate any modelling of writing.

For our very young pupils in KS1, we provide ample sentence stems that will support them in disciplinary writing; in fact, we do this all the way through to Year 6, especially to support any of our lower prior-attaining pupils. As we build up our pupils' stamina for extended writing, to begin we may provide them with the topic sentence and concluding sentence for each paragraph (a technique highlighted in *The Writing Revolution* by Judith C. Hochman and Natalie Wexler, 2017). This scaffold is gradually removed as pupils gain confidence by Year 6.

Table 8.2 Scaffolding example

Question: What motivated Britain to build an empire?	
Global Trade	**Topic sentence**: Britain wanted to trade and import goods that could not be grown at home.
	Point 1: ....
	Point 2: ....
	Point 3: ....
	Concluding sentence: Overall, engaging in global trade played a significant role in shaping the British Empire and influencing its economy.

Oral outcomes are prioritised for SEND learners. Some of our SEND adaptations enable pupils to learn about history, geography and science in a multisensory way. For example, when learning about archaeology, a sand tray with artifacts and a paintbrush might be provided for pupils with more moderate learning needs to experience the content tactilely.

Case study example: Knowledge School Trust, disciplinary literacy

What is your approach to oracy? What are your thoughts on subject-specific or disciplinary oracy?

From EYFS to Year 6, every lesson across the curriculum includes a 'Talk Task' specifically designed to support the knowledge objectives. These tasks are often modelled with an adult, and sentence stems are provided to scaffold pupil responses. These tasks will also directly link to the independent task so that pupils can practice verbally saying what they will be independently writing about.

The Education Endowment Foundation (EEF) published a report in 2019, 'Improving Literacy in Secondary Schools', emphasising the importance of disciplinary literacy and structured talk in developing students' writing skills. The report highlights the need for explicit instruction in the specific language and conventions used in different subject areas, enabling pupils to communicate their understanding effectively. This is echoed in 'Improving Literacy in KS2', published in 2021. Additionally, the EEF report stresses the value of talk in the writing process. Structured discussions and activities that encourage pupils to articulate their ideas and receive feedback from peers and teachers can significantly enhance their writing abilities. By incorporating both disciplinary literacy instruction and talk-based strategies, educators can provide comprehensive support for students' writing development. However, as is echoed by Clare Sealy, the way in which we speak is different from the standard English expectations we apply when creating a piece of formal writing, which is why many of our written resources need to be clear subject-specific models that can be utilised by our pupils to give them a clear picture of what writing in the subject is structured.

In addition to 'Talk Tasks', every lesson from EYFS to Year 6 has an explicit 'vocabulary' section. During this part of the lesson, pupils are asked to orally rehearse the key vocabulary and often (or when appropriate) the words are accompanied by an action. This simple task allows all our pupils, especially our SEND, EAL and lower prior attaining pupils, to orally practise saying the key words out loud with their peers. These words will then be up on our working walls and will be up during the 'Talk Task' part of our lesson so that pupils have another opportunity to purposefully apply their new vocabulary.

Further to this, we encourage teachers to utilise 'talk partners' little and often throughout a lesson, so that by the end of an hour lesson, pupils have had ample opportunity to discuss any prior learning or new learning with their peers. Once pupils have begun writing, teachers would often select pupils to read their examples aloud to their peers, building their public speaking confidence. The act of doing this can often also prompt our pupils to notice any mistakes in their writing, so that they can then immediately correct them.

During any whole class discussions, we have also utilised Doug Lemov's habits of discussion technique and Lauren Resnick's (2018) work on accountable talk. In our trust, we teach the pupils three simple sentences stems *'I agree with X because...'*, *'I disagree with X because...'* and *'Building on X's response...'*. Embedding these into the classroom culture means that pupils not only have to listen carefully to what the teacher is saying, but also to their peers and their responses, thoughts and ideas.

What advice would you give to schools if they want to implement disciplinary literacy and oracy?

- Develop your own understanding of disciplinary knowledge across the breadth of subjects.
- Focus on developing staff's disciplinary knowledge and understanding first.
- Then focus on developing staff's understanding of disciplinary literacy.
- Develop staff's confidence in understanding the nuance between history, geography and scientific writing, and show examples and non-examples.
- Audit the tasks teachers are setting across the subjects and ask: Do they match the subject discipline? Or are they unintentionally distracting pupils from thinking about things that are not necessary or accurate for that subject? (e.g. writing a diary entry from the perspective of a hunter-gatherer).
- Monitoring the resources teachers make and provide specific feedback to them on what is working and what needs tweaking.

Case study example: Knowledge School Trust, disciplinary literacy

- Monitor pupil outcomes; ask: 'What common errors or misconceptions do pupils (or the staff) hold? What is going well? What further CPD support do staff need?'.

Recommended reading from Juli Ryzop

Counsell, C. (2018) Taking curriculum seriously. https://my.chartered.college/impact_article/taking-curriculum-seriously/ (Accessed: 04/04/2025)

Sealy, C. (2023) Talking Floats On A Sea Of Write. https://hwrkmagazine.co.uk/talking-floats-on-a-sea-of-write/ (Accessed: 04/04/2025)

Sealy, C. (2024) Oracies not oracy. https://primarytimery.com/2024/08/25/oracies-not-oracy/ (Accessed: 04/04/2025)

Disciplinary writing at PKC

Disciplinary history examples:

https://x.com/PKCKST/status/1869488307077251525 (Accessed: 04/04/2025)

Chapter 9:
Disciplinary literacy across the curriculum

Disciplinary-appropriate writing in maths leads to stronger mathematical reasoning and use of mathematical vocabulary by 7-year-olds

(Cohen, Casa, Miller and Firmender, 2015, in Shanahan, 2019)

Across all subjects, there are opportunities for pupils to speak and think within a particular subject discipline. Mathematics has had the most research (Shanahan, 2019 and Croce, 2024), especially with a focus on talking in mathematics. However, other subjects can focus on understanding and developing strong disciplinary knowledge so that pupils can deepen their knowledge of a particular subject through talk. For example, exploring and critiquing art in the primary classroom is a skill that will support pupils in the future, but can be developed orally in primary schools.

Disciplinary literacy in mathematics

This section will focus solely on thinking and speaking like a mathematician, as this will be appropriate for the primary classroom and the EYFS environment. Both exploratory talk and accountable talk are equally applicable to mathematics in developing disciplinary knowledge. The question below (Figure 9.1) is taken from the 2024 KS2 national curriculum paper (commonly known as SATs) and 15% of pupils across the country answered it correctly. When reading in mathematics, the focus is not always on finding the correct answer but on reasoning and problem-solving skills. It not only requires pupils to read the question like a mathematician, but it also requires a written and reasoned response, which justifies the statement for one mark. In this example, they are not looking for an answer but for a reason why Olivia is correct, requiring a detailed and written explanation.

Figure 9.1 Example question; Olivia has two jars of beads

Source: KS2 mathematics national curriculum test 2024. Reasoning paper 2. Contains material developed by the Standards and Testing Agency for 2024 national curriculum assessments and licensed under Open Government Licence v3.0.

Chapter 9: Disciplinary literacy across the curriculum

Here is an example of how pupils and teachers might read in mathematics.

Reading comprehension strategies	Make predictions	Visualise	Ask questions	Make connections	Clarify	Summarise and evaluate
Mathematics (Problem solving and reasoning)	Think about whether you have completed a problem like this before. What is the best strategy? Make estimates.	Write out the calculation. Use concrete, abstract and pictorial strategies. Use columns etc.	Has this improved my understanding of the question? Are there any other strategies I need to remember?	Does this link to other problems I have solved? Can I use known facts, e.g. doubles, halves or number bonds?	Check calculations. What are the key words I need to know?	Think about how well you have answered the question.

Adapted from: Quigley, A., Muijs, D. & Stringer, E. (2021b)

Example explanation

Olivia has two jars of beads *[Predictions: 'Have I seen a question like this before? I remember learning about beads. I need to remember she has two jars.']*

The number of beads in Jar A is double the number of beads in Jar B. *[Estimate: 'I know that double is going to be twice as much. So Jar A is two times bigger.' Visualise: 'I can see that the jar should be half the size. Although it does look a bit different in the picture, I am going to use what I have read.]*

Olivia says *[Ask questions and make connections]*: *'I know that 25% x 4 is 100% and I know my doubles and halves. If there are 100 beads in Jar A and 50 beads in Jar B because it is half the size, 25% of A is 25 which is the same as 50% of 50. 50% is double 25% so 50% of a half is equal to 25% of a whole.']*

Explain why Olivia is correct.

1 mark *[Clarify]*, 'I have checked the calculations using what I know about doubles and halves. I have explained my reasons.'

Questions like this further exemplify the importance of 'accountable talk' (Michaels et al, 2010) or similar, and giving pupils the opportunity to justify their answers with evidence to back up any claims, as well using metacognitive talk to process the questions.

- 'What do you mean exactly?'
- 'Do you agree with this answer. Why or why not?'
- 'Would anyone like to build on this answer?
- 'What mathematical knowledge have you drawn on?' Pupils will need to draw on their knowledge of doubling and halving.

Pupils would have been awarded a mark for correctly explaining that the two quantities are equal. For example (from the mark scheme):

'If there are 100 beads in Jar A and 50 beads in Jar B, 25% of A is 25 which is the same as 50% of 50. 50% is double 25% so 50% of a half is equal to 25% of a whole'.

'A quarter equals half of a half.'

Diagrams as part of an explanation if they show clearly that 50% of the half is equal to 25% of the whole (see Figure 9.2).

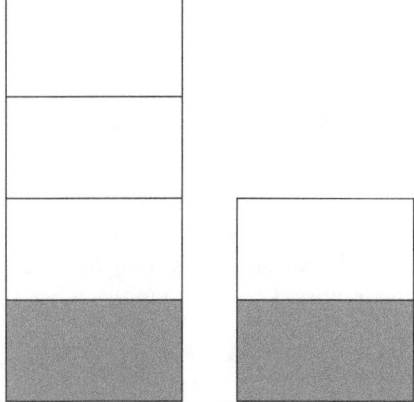

Figure 9.2 Visual explanation of the answer

Marks are not awarded for answers that reinstate the question.

'Because Jar B is half the amount of Jar A.'

'25 + 25 = 50'

Interestingly, pupils need to have mathematical knowledge to fully participate in mathematical talk.

Speaking and thinking like a mathematician (problem solving focus)

EYFS (Prompts for adults)	I know… so I also know… The patterns are like… I can show this idea by… The numbers remind me of… I see that… I want to know…
KS1	I can prove my thinking by… A better strategy would be… If I worked this out again I would… My mistake happened when… I can use the inverse of… to check… I realised that… so I…
KS2	To test my hypothesis, I could… I predict… because… When I estimate my answer, I get… The most efficient method would be… I approached this problem by… I would use this in real life when…

(Sentence stems created by Natasha Dolling, primary mathematics specialist, LEO Academy Trust)

EYFS examples

Examples	Adult modelling and questioning
I want to know…	'I want to know if I squeeze this sponge, will it stay small.'
I see that…	'I see that there are 2 here and 2 there so there must be 4.' 'I see that Jade has more hoops than Ahmed.'

Disciplinary literacy in primary schools

Figure 9.3, Question: What is 47 + 72, answer =119

Who has made an error?

Similarly to history, using Who? What? When? Where? Why? as a structure for developing oral and written explanations is a particularly powerful method for pupils. Using words, such as *'I know this because...'* is also a very helpful scaffold for pupils. Hochman et al (2024) use this structure across the curriculum to develop and expand sentences.

Direction: expand the sentence

Who made an error?

Who? Arnav

When? Adding the 4+2 instead of 40+2. He should have added 7+2.

Why? Confused with place value.

Expanded sentence: Arnav made a mistake because he added 4+2 instead of 7+2. He was confused with place value.

Direction: expand the sentence

Who made an error?

Who? Josh

When? Adding 4+7 instead of 40+70.

Why? Did not understand place value.

Expanded sentence: Josh made a mistake because he added 4+7 instead of 40+70. He did not understand place value.

Disciplinary literacy links to being a skilled mathematician

Louise Pennington (Head of Professional Development at Oxford University Press and mathematics specialist) has developed a disciplinary literacy approach that fits in appropriately with the mathematical proficiency reading rope developed by Kilpatrick et al in 2001 in their instrumental publication called, *Adding it Up.*

It consists of five strands that show different aspects of mathematical proficiency.

Strand	Explanation Kilpatrick et al (2001)	Links to thinking and reading like a mathematician – problem solving and reasoning
Conceptual understanding	Comprehension of mathematical concepts, operations and relations.	Know the 'why' and 'when' when solving mathematical problems. For example, using 'who', 'why', and 'when'.
Procedural fluency	Skill in carrying out procedures flexibly, accurately, efficiently and appropriately.	Be flexible and efficient and reflect on the strategies used.
Strategic competence	Ability to formulate, represent and solve mathematical problems.	Show and explain calculations through visual representations.
Adaptive reasoning	Capacity for logical thought, reflection, explanation and justification.	Pupils need to reflect, explain and justify their answers.
Productive disposition	Habitual inclination to see mathematics as sensible, useful and worthwhile, coupled with a belief in diligence and one's own efficacy.	Pupils should draw on their declaration knowledge, e.g. *I know that 5 x10 is 50 so I also know that 50 x10 = 500.*

(Adapted by Louise Pennington)

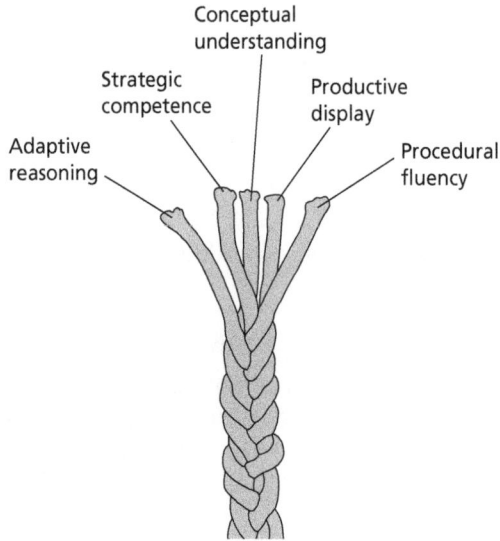

Figure 9.3 Intertwined strands of proficiency

Pupil-friendly examples

What makes a good mathematician? NRICH blog. https://nrich.maths.org/what-makes-good-mathematician (Accessed 04/04/2025)

Further reading

NCETM (2023). Reasoning through talk. www.ncetm.org.uk/media/4rrfsgtl/reasoning-ofsted-report-final.pdf (Accessed 04/04/2025)

NRICH (2011). Using Questioning to Stimulate Mathematical Thinking. https://nrich.maths.org/articles/using-questioning-stimulate-mathematical-thinking (Accessed 04/04/2025)

Oxford University Press (2024). Talk for mathematics. https://fdslive.oup.com/www.oup.com/oxed/primary/maths/OUP_TalkforMathsBenchmarks_2024.pdf?region=uk (Accessed 04/04/2025)

Doing and talking math and science. Blog. A resource to support talking in mathematics and science. https://stem4els.wceruw.org/resources.html (Accessed 04/04/2025)

NRICH. Visualising and representing. https://nrich.maths.org/visualising-and-representing-primary-teachers (Accessed 04/04/2025)

Disciplinary literacy in religious education (RE)

The RE curriculum rarely enabled pupils to systematically build disciplinary knowledge or personal knowledge.

(Ofsted, 2024)

According to Ofsted (2021) there are three types of knowledge in RE that pupils need to have a broad understanding of RE. However, these are rarely explored in depth during RE lessons. The types of knowledge are:

1. Substantive knowledge: knowledge about various religious and non-religious traditions.
2. Ways of knowing: pupils learn 'how to know' about religion and non-religion. This can be broken down into theology, philosophy and sociology.
3. Personal knowledge: pupils build an awareness of their own presuppositions and values about the religious and non-religious traditions they study.

('Ways of knowing in practice', Ofsted, 2021)

How have different Muslims understood sacred texts about Tawhid? (A 'theology' question.)

Is the idea of God's self-existence a coherent one? (A 'philosophy' question.)

What is the significance of Tawhid for the way that different Muslims live today? (A 'sociology' question.)

Substantive concepts

- Different ways that people express religion and non-religion in their lives, including diverse lived experiences and the complexity of the fluid boundaries between different traditions.
- Knowledge about artefacts and texts associated with different religious and non-religious traditions.
- Concepts that relate to religious and non-religious traditions, such as 'dharma', 'incarnation', 'ritual', 'authority', 'prayer', 'sacred', 'anatta' and 'moksha'.
- The very concepts of 'religion' and 'non-religion' and debates around these ideas.

(Ofsted, 2021)

These are clearly defined Ofsted terms which link in successfully with similar terminology used in history and other subjects. One of Ofsted's (2024) key recommendation is to, 'Make sure that curriculums clearly identify how pupils will develop disciplinary and personal knowledge through the chosen substantive content.' This information is relevant to religious education, because to understand disciplinary literacy, we need to understand what is and is not RE knowledge and understanding.

Speaking in RE: examples that incorporate disciplinary knowledge

Religious education	Reception This festival is important because… This text/story teaches us [religious text]… This is important to [religious group] because… I would do this… **Key Stage 1** Many people from this [religious group] do this because… This text/story teaches us… about this religion… This text tells me that this [religious group] believes that… This is important to this [religious group] because… This [religious group] acts in this way because… I would… in this situation. **Key Stage 2** Many people from this [religious group] do this because… This artefact/text/story teaches us… about this religion… This text tells me that this [religious group] believes that… This is important to this religious group because… Many people in this religious group would do… in this situation… I would do this… This religious group acts in this way because… I would… in this situation…

These language frames are useful when exploring religious stories, but also for considering when we read and write in RE.

Chapter 9: Disciplinary literacy across the curriculum

Reading comprehension strategies	Make predictions	Visualise	Ask questions	Make connections	Clarify	Summarise and evaluate
Religious education	Have you read a text/book artefact like this before? Does this link to any other religious stories/texts?	Imagine the narrative in your head.	What does this teach us? How do this group view this situation? Why is this important to this religious group?	What would you do in this situation?	Discuss the meaning of unfamiliar words, e.g. 'resurrection'.	Write down three things you have learnt from this text/story.

Jesus's followers mourned the loss of their teacher and leader *[Make predictions: I remember learning about Christmas last year. I can see that Jesus is no longer around because it says, 'mourned'].* But on the third day, something extraordinary happened that would change the course of history. Early on that Sunday morning, some women went to Jesus's tomb, only to find it empty *[Visualise: I can see the tomb which will be very old as this was a long time ago].* An angel appeared and told them the astonishing news *[Make connections: In this situation, I think I would be completely surprised, but very hopeful]*: Jesus had risen from the dead and was resurrected! *[Clarify: I need to double-check what this means. Ask questions: I wonder how Christians feel about this as an important event.]* Overwhelmed with joy and disbelief, they rushed to tell the others. *[Summarise: Jesus had died. Jesus was missing from the tomb. Jesus was found alive.]*

Talk time examples

Jesus's followers mourned the loss of their teacher and leader. But on the third day, something extraordinary happened that would change the course of history. Early on that Sunday morning, some women went to Jesus's tomb, only to find it empty. An angel appeared and told them the astonishing news: Jesus had risen from the dead! Overwhelmed with joy and disbelief, they rushed to tell the others.

Discussion points:

What does the Easter story teach Christians?

Sentence stems

This story tells me that Christians believe that…

This is important to Christians because…

Unlike history, geography and science, schools might not write extended essays in RE, although many do. However, I have seen this in some faith schools and the focus is primarily on the discipline of RE as opposed to generic English skills, e.g. retelling a religious story. The substantive and disciplinary knowledge shown above should be evident in the work that pupils produce. Again, this is not necessarily about quantity but about the quality of the writing or work that the pupils are encouraged to produce.

Let's look at the two examples below:

Easter – example 1

Jesus's followers mourned the loss of their teacher and leader. But on the third day, something extraordinary happened that would change the course of history. Early on that Sunday morning, some women went to Jesus's tomb, only to find it empty. An angel appeared and told them the astonishing news: Jesus had risen from the dead! Overwhelmed with joy and disbelief, they rushed to tell the others.

Easter – example 2

The Easter story is important to Christians because it reminds them that there is always a possibility of new life and that through faith, we can overcome many obstacles.

Example 1 is simply a retelling of the Easter story, which might be very appropriate for very young pupils and enable them to recall and discuss the story. However, example 2 supports pupils to explore the Easter story through a disciplinary lens and enables them to think deeply about what this might mean to Christians. [I note that in some Church schools, they might use 'us' as opposed to 'Christians'.] Although shorter, example 2 demonstrates a pupil's understanding of the content and knowledge needed within RE.

References and bibliography

Croce, K. A. (2024) Disciplinary literacy in mathematics. In Ortleib, E, Kane, E.D., and Cheek, E.H. *Disciplinary Literacies: Unpacking Research, Theory, and Practice*, 36–54.

Education Endowment Foundation (2022). Improving mathematics in Key Stages 2 and 3. https://educationendowmentfoundation.org.uk/education-evidence/guidance-reports/maths-ks-2-3 (Accessed: 04/04/2025)

Enderson, M. C. & Colwell, J. (2021) Considering possibilities to promote disciplinary literacy instruction in mathematics. *Journal of Adolescent & Adult Literacy*, 64(6), 683–692.

Hager, G. (2018) *Disciplinary Literacy in the Mathematics Classroom*. Mathematics Education Research Group of Australasia.

Hochman, J. C. & Wexler, N. (2024) *The Writing Revolution 2.0: A Guide to Advancing Thinking Through Writing in All Subjects and Grades*. Wiley.

Kane, B. D., Robinson, R. J., Blanton, M. S. & Albert, J. (2024) Letting the Mathematics Lead in Mathematical Literacy: Toward an Understanding of Literacy in Mathematics. In *Cultivating Literate Citizenry Through Interdisciplinary Instruction* (pp. 94–115). IGI Global.

Lent, R. C. & Voigt, M. M. (2018) *Disciplinary Literacy in Action: How to Create and Sustain a School-Wide Culture of Deep Reading, Writing, and Thinking*. SAGE Publications.

Michaels, S., O'Connor, C. & Williams-Hall, M. C., with Resnick, L. B. (2010) *Accountable Talk Sourcebook: For Classroom Conversation That Works*. Institute for Learning, University of Pittsburgh.

NCETM (2022). Four ways to create better mathematical talk in your classroom. www.ncetm.org.uk/features/four-ways-to-create-better-mathematical-talk-in-your-classroom/ (Accessed: 04/04/2025)

Kilpatrick, J., Swafford, J. & Findell, B. (Eds.) (2001) *Adding it up: Helping Children Learn Mathematics*. National Research Council.

Ofsted (2021) Research review series: religious education. www.gov.uk/government/publications/research-review-series-religious-education/research-review-series-religious-education#curriculum-progression (Accessed: 04/04/2025)

Ofsted (2024) Research and analysis. Deep and meaningful? The religious education subject report. www.gov.uk/government/publications/subject-report-series-religious-education/deep-and-meaningful-the-religious-education-subject-report (Accessed: 04/04/2025)

Chapter 10
Case study example:
Implementing disciplinary literacy across an academy trust with Shareen Wilkinson

Multi-Academy Trust: LEO Academy Trust

CEO: Phillip Hedger

Trust Curriculum Lead and Executive Director of Education: Shareen Wilkinson

Trust Professional Learning Lead and Assistant Director of Education: Amy Carlile

Background

LEO Academy Trust serves over 6000 pupils from across Sutton (London) and Surrey. The trust was formed in 2015 and since then, we have developed a family of great learning communities formed from currently 12 primary schools.

With over 700+ staff, our schools are empowered to support each other to improve both outcomes for our pupils, and to drive performance across the wider school system. We are a high performing trust with a focus on learning, digital skills and extensive curriculum enrichment opportunities, including sport, music, art and drama, and strive for educational excellence for all our pupils, especially those with special educational needs and the most disadvantaged.

Staff received central training on disciplinary literacy but across LEO Academy Trust the curriculum is different, so they had to personalise disciplinary literacy to the needs of their individual schools and provide their own staff training based on resources provided centrally.

Case study school examples

- Cheam Common Infant and Junior Academy (LEO Academy Trust).
- Brookfield Primary Academy (LEO Academy Trust).
- Manor Park Primary Academy (LEO Academy Trust).

Key texts

Back in 2020, I attended a training session led by Professor Timothy Shanahan on Disciplinary Literacy in Primary Schools (organised by Greenshaw Learning Trust). This was the event that sparked my curiosity and inspired me to implement this in local schools (through training) as well as LEO Academy Trust.

The main research that prompted my interest in disciplinary literacy was this one, written for the Irish curriculum:

Shanahan, T. (2019) Disciplinary Literacy in Primary Schools. https://ncca.ie/media/4679/disciplinary-literacy-in-the-primary-school-professor-timothy-shanahan-university-of-illinois-at-chicago-1.pdf (Accessed: 04/04/25)

Others include:

- *Disciplinary Literacy and Explicit Vocabulary Instruction* by Katherine Mortimore
- *Closing the Vocabulary Gap* by Alex Quigley
- *Closing the Reading Gap* by Alex Quigley
- *A Dialogic Teaching Companion* by Robin Alexander
- *The Writing Revolution 2* by Judith C Hochman and Natalie Wexler (2024)
- 'Improving Literacy in Secondary Schools' by the EEF (2019)

Case study example: implementing disciplinary literacy across an academy trust

- *Accountable Talk* by Lauren Resnik et al (2018)
- Lent, R. C., Voigt, M. M. (2018) *Disciplinary Literacy in Action: How to Create and Sustain a School-Wide Culture of Deep Reading, Writing, and Thinking.*
- Sharples, J., Eaton, J. and Boughelaf, J. (2024) 'A School's Guide to Implementation'. Education Endowment Foundation.

How did we support staff?

- Initially, I introduced disciplinary literacy to principals and headteachers, focusing on its definition and the subtle distinctions between writing in history, geography and science.
- Inspired by Mary Myatt's work on stories in the curriculum, I collaborated with one of our schools (Brookfield Primary Academy) to develop a list of curriculum books that support schema building. This was based on research by Professor Daniel Willingham, who found that we remember more when information is presented within a story.
- A year later, I provided training to all central team education staff, explaining different knowledge types, such as substantive and disciplinary knowledge. I emphasised that substantive knowledge refers to the key facts, concepts and information within a subject domain – the foundational building blocks of understanding. Disciplinary knowledge on the other hand, encompasses the specialised skills and procedures used by experts within a field to investigate, analyse and communicate ideas. I highlighted that this distinction was crucial to grasp before effectively implementing disciplinary literacy across the curriculum, ensuring that pupils not only acquire essential content but also develop the tools to think and work like practitioners within each subject area.
- We established writing networks for each year group (Reception to Year 6) and I trained writing facilitators in disciplinary writing. This ensured every year group across the trust (including other local schools) had knowledge and understanding of disciplinary writing and its significance.

- I conducted training sessions for curriculum leads and senior leaders across LEO primary schools, specifically addressing disciplinary writing, reading, thinking and speaking.
- Over two years, I collaborated with teachers and subject leaders to create original 'Speak like a...' posters. These posters aimed to help pupils understand key subject-specific skills and utilise them in discussions as a scaffold. They were designed for pupils from Early Years Foundation Stage to Year 6 and involved attending training with subject specialists over a two-year period. For instance, I attended training provided by the Historical Association and the Geographical Association.

What does it look like now?

Most schools complete a piece of extended disciplinary writing once every six weeks for science, geography and history. This entails three pieces of writing from each subject a year. This is primarily from Year 2 onwards, with Year 1 completing their work in lessons. Science is typically completed within science lessons and the other subjects are completed during the last week, during the English lesson time. That way, pupils produce high quality writing in the subject disciplines, which are of similar quality to English writing. In other subjects, the focus is on oral discussions in class where pupils speak like mathematicians or artists.

Examples:

Disciplinary writing across LEO Academy Trust. https://x.com/ShareenAdvice/status/1793202375265583481

Use of technology

Across the trust, all schools utilise digital skills as part of the trust teaching and learning and digital strategy, so that technology is used to enhance teaching and learning. It is used across all subjects and is equally beneficial for feedback and response on disciplinary writing and pupils' work. Indeed, disciplinary writing does not always have to be written in books and could be presented in different ways where appropriate, e.g. oral presentations, slides, recordings etc.

Digital tool/method	Examples of effective use for feedback and response
Multimedia presentations	Address misconceptions, showcase pupil work, facilitate peer assessment, pinpoint pupils needing support.
Digital quizzing	Gain real-time insights into whole-class performance.
Screen recordings	Provide visual cues, offer dynamic explanations, create a more engaging experience, enable flexible learning.
Screen casting	Foster collaboration, personalise feedback.
Voice recordings	Convey warmth, empathy and encouragement.
Google classroom (or equivalent)	Utilise comments for personalised feedback, provide instant verbal feedback, collaborate on documents.

Further reading:

Aubrey-Smith, F. & Twining, P. (2023) *From EdTech to PedTech: Changing the Way We Think about Digital Technology*. Taylor & Francis.

Examples from LEO Academy Trust Schools

Cheam Common Junior Academy

Cheam Common Junior Academy is situated in Cheam and is a part of LEO Academy Trust. They have fully implemented disciplinary writing into their writing curriculum. Writing tasks are used for pupils to demonstrate their knowledge and understanding of six weeks' learning.

Here are some examples of their practice:

Curriculum dictionaries support the whole class with understanding key vocabulary across the curriculum. All pupils can contribute to this dictionary.

As with any writing lesson, pupils are exposed to **high quality examples** of geography writing and explore the key features, before planning and writing their own. They use banners to support the pupils with key vocabulary and a success criteria focused on the subject discipline for geography. This is not about assessing English but the knowledge in science, history and geography that they have acquired after typically six weeks of learning.

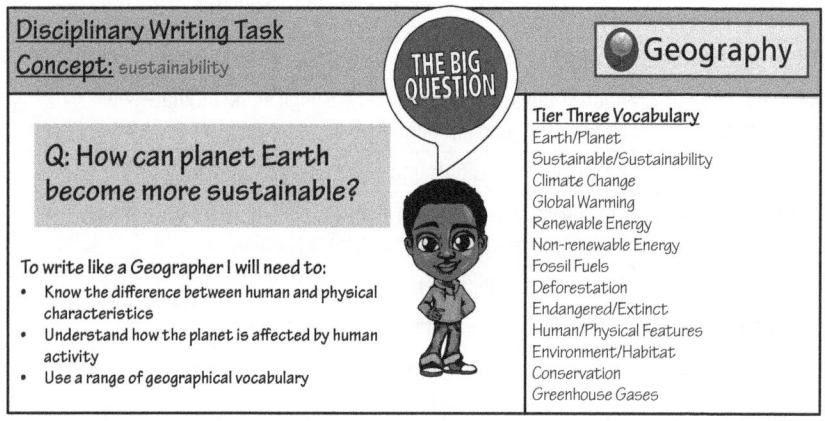

Figure 10.1 Geography writing task

(Source: Artwork and design by Julaan Govier, curriculum lead at Cheam Common Junior Academy)

Organisation of disciplinary writing each term at Cheam Common Junior Academy

This table shows how Cheam Common Junior Academy have organised their disciplinary writing across the academic year. However, LEO Academy Trust schools vary in how often they complete a piece of extended disciplinary writing. This ranges from one piece of geography, history or science writing a year to one piece per term (or three pieces of history, geography or science writing a year). Schools also provide opportunities to write about what they have learnt in history in their English books. For example, writing diaries or letters from the viewpoint of historically significant characters.

Case study example: implementing disciplinary literacy across an academy trust

Table 10.1 Disciplinary writing for each term

Curriculum book This should be completed in the morning and show what pupils know and understand.			
	Autumn	Spring	Summer
Year 3	History – Stone Age Question: **How did life change for people from the Stone Age to the Iron Age?** Concept: **change and continuity** (from the Stone Age to the Iron Age	Geography – Volcanoes Question: **What impact do volcanic eruptions have on humans?** Concept; **Environment**	History – Ancient Egyptians Question: **How did Howard Carter's discovery of Tutankhamun's tomb help us to learn more about the Ancient Egyptians** Concept(s) **Use of evidence. Interpret evidence and communicate ideas**
Year 4	History – Romans Question: **How did the achievements of the Romans in Britain impact modern life?** Concept: **Significance**	Geography – Rainforests Question; **Why are rainforests important to the world?** Concept: **Environment**	History – Vikings Question: **Why did the Vikings come to Britain?** Concept: Reflection, Trade
Year 5	Science – Space Question: **How does Planet Earth sustain life for humanity** Concept: **Research. Interpreting and Communicating Results**	Geography Green Schools Project – Sustainability Question: **How can Planet Earth become more sustainable?** Concept: **Sustainability**	Geography (Science) Question: **How are rivers connected to the water cycle?** Concept: **Interconnections**
Year 6	Geography – Trade Question: **Is 'globalisation' a positive or a negative?** Concept(s) **Interconnectedness and Environment**	History – WW2 Question: **What was the impact of WW2 on the people of Britain?** Concept: **Significance**	Science – Cardiology Question: **How do you keep your heart healthy?** Concept(s): **Research. Interpreting and Communicating Results**

Example of disciplinary writing at Cheam Common Junior Academy: https://x.com/2ndry_Teacher/status/1783119746449232304

Speaking and listening

Pupils at Cheam Common Infant and Junior Academy engage in extensive discussions and are competent and able to debate, using scaffolds and symbols, such as, *'I would like to build on XXX point.'* These scaffolds support pupils to think critically and consider all options. The school, alongside other LEO schools, has extensive apps that support pupils with their access to reading and writing. This enables pupils who would not normally speak in class to record themselves and gives them dignity in learning.

Brookfield Primary Academy

Brookfield Primary Academy is in Sutton, south London and is a part of LEO Academy Trust.

The school has really focused on ensuring the pupils peer and self-assess their disciplinary writing. Pupils are encouraged to use subject-specific feedback, rather than focussing on grammar and punctuation. This is, of course, important but the focus should be on the content of the writing.

First draft	Improvements after feedback
From undertaking the noise level...	From analysing the noise level...

One critique of disciplinary writing is the level of independence of the writing. However, at Brookfield they focus on showing excellent examples and like any English lesson, gradually release so that pupils can show what they know and can do. Ultimately, the writing will read differently across a class.

At Brookfield, they use 'Read Aloud' books to develop rich schemata and it was the school that I initially trialled the lists below in. Reading

Case study example: implementing disciplinary literacy across an academy trust

aloud takes places across the week and is fully timetabled. This enables teachers to model excellent fluency and use strategies (where appropriate) such as echo reading and choral reading. Reading across the curriculum enables pupils to build the background knowledge and research needed for their writing and discussions across the curriculum.

Suggested year group	Books	Links
Nursery/Reception	*Coming to England* by Floella Benjamin	Builds up the substantive concept of monarchy. Useful for looking at historical significance in year 1.
Reception	*Martha Maps* in *Out* by Leigh Hodgkinson	Builds up geographical map skills. Useful for looking at wider maps in the future.
Year 1	*The Great Fire of London* by Amy Adams	Prepares pupils for more formal study in year 2.
Year 2	*Moth* by Isabel Thomas	Prepares pupils for studying evolution in KS2.
Year 3	*River story* by Meridith Hopper	Links to topic on rivers – supporting background knowledge.
Year 4	*Overheard in a Tower Block* by Joseph Coelho	Supports pupils with understanding place in geography.
Year 5	*Hidden Figures* by Margaret Lee Shetterley	Explores historical significance and links to studying space.
Year 6	*Charles Darwin's Origin of Species* by Sabina Radeva	Great for studying evolution in science.

Brookfield also use books to introduce key concepts across the curriculum during curriculum lessons. For example, a book on the current monarch might be useful when introducing the topic of monarchy so that pupils can fully engage with a topic. This is typically carried out at the start of a unit of work.

At Brookfield Primary Academy they have explicitly planned for talk opportunities across the curriculum. This overview enables structured talk to be planned for and relates to speaking and writing across the disciplines.

Example of disciplinary geography writing at Brookfield: https://x.com/ShareenAdvice/status/1773357642431283374

Example of disciplinary history writing at Brookfield: https://x.com/ShareenAdvice/status/1783492440512410074

Manor Park Primary Academy

Manor Park Primary Academy uses structured talk time to discuss key concepts and deepen knowledge and understanding. They also use stories to introduce key concepts within the foundation subjects.

Science – Year 2 at Manor Park Primary Academy, part of LEO Academy Trust

Today we are going to explain and describe each stage of our chosen life cycle.

> Talk time
>
> We need to think and speak like a scientist.
>
> This diagram shows...
>
> At this stage, the diagram shows...
>
> Explain the stages to your partner. Remember to use scientific vocabulary.

Assessment in geography, history or science is based on the substantive and disciplinary knowledge that the pupils have acquired. Therefore, feedback and next steps are based on this.

Tips for implementation

- Make sure that English is taught well first before embarking on disciplinary writing.
- It is important for EYFS and KS1 pupils to get their foundational (handwriting, spelling, composition) knowledge right first. Therefore, only start disciplinary writing when your pupils are ready and competent at the basics.
- Use disciplinary writing where it fits in rather than changing everything.
- Review curriculum planning to see where there are opportunities to embed disciplinary literacy strategies.
- Ensure disciplinary writing is age and stage appropriate.
- Provide opportunities for curriculum subject leaders to gain sufficient subject knowledge. Engaging with the subject associations is a good starting point, e.g. the Historical or Geographical Associations.
- Use great example texts of disciplinary writing.
- All subjects need to have a clear progression map, so that knowledge and skills are built up over time. This must start from early years so that pupils are prepared for their next steps.
- Invest time in training teachers so that they are knowledgeable about the different subjects.
- Involve staff in creating resources and review implementation at each stage.

Appendix:
Disciplinary literacy in other subjects

All these sentence stems were written based on the disciplinary knowledge that pupils need to know and understand within each subject discipline, based on the national curriculum 2014 and Ofsted research guidance. They support teachers and pupils to know what it means to think and read within the subject and the content of the writing if it is focused on the discipline.

Sentence stems for speaking across the subject disciplines

Art	**Early Years Foundation Stage** The materials I used are… The tools I used to make it were… I like/dislike this artwork because… It makes me feel… The materials the artist used are… **Key stage 1** The tools the artist used to make it were… The similarities and differences are… It makes me feel…because… The materials the artist used are…because… I was inspired by… The skills that helped me create this are… The artist is important because… **Key stage 2** I mastered the technique by… The materials I used to develop the technique are… I reviewed and developed my artwork by… The artist that inspired me was… I experimented with… My design process included…

Appendix: Disciplinary literacy in other subjects

Music	**Early Years Foundation Stage** I can hear sounds that are [really loud/very quiet]. I [enjoy/don't enjoy] this music because… This music makes me feel… This music is [quick/slow]. I like the way the [instrument] sounds. I can play the [instrument]. **Key stage 1** I like the sound the [instrument] makes because… The music makes me feel…because… I enjoy playing the [instrument] because… I chose these instruments because… This song/piece of music is [like/unlike] the other one because… **Key stage 2** This part of the song/music makes me think of… I [enjoy/don't enjoy] this type of music because… This composer/musician is inspiring because… My composition was inspired by…. I particularly like how the composer uses… I included…in the melody I created because… The lyrics in this song are about/remind me of… I can write music down using…
Design and technology	**Early Years Foundation Stage** I have made this because… Next time I could… I am using these tools because… I have used this material because… **Key stage 1** My purpose for this design is… I have chosen these tools and this equipment because… I have chosen these materials because… My ideas are… My evaluation of this product is… **Key stage 2** My product is fit for purpose because… My research has helped with this design because… I have selected these tools/ materials because… My analysis and evaluation of this product is… I could improve my design by…

PSHE	[These sentence stems focus on the social and emotional aspect of citizenship.] **Early Years Foundation Stage** I have tried... I am not giving up. I feel happy/sad/angry/worried because... I think that... I share and play with... I wash my hands when... I can do this! [Linked to executive function] **Key stage 1** I think that...because... I would like to challenge that because ... I would like to build on... I feel happy/sad/angry/worried because... I am responsible because... I show kindness to others by... **Key stage 2** I overcame this challenge by... I learn from my mistakes and never give up. I listened to [XXX] perspective when... I am considerate of others when... I agree with your point... I would like to build on... I would like to challenge... I disagree because...

Appendix: Disciplinary literacy in other subjects

PE (Text created by Matt Warner, Director of Sport and PE at LEO Academy Trust)	[These sentence stems focus on disciplinary knowledge in PE.] **Early Years Foundation Stage** I'm sharing my toys with my friends. I'm listening to my teacher. I can do it like you, look. Look how fast I can move! I can feel my heart moving when... I'm careful when I play... **Key stage 1** I have practised... You're doing great, keep going! I can improve by... Watch me move. I'll keep trying until I can do it! I can feel my heart pumping! **Key stage 2** Let's make it more challenging! My strategy is going to be to... We can improve by doing ... I am resilient. I never give up! I'm pushing myself and improving. We make a great team!

Benefits of disciplinary literacy

Disciplinary literacy offers a range of benefits for both pupils and teaching staff when implemented in the classroom and across the curriculum. It equips pupils with the specialised skills and knowledge required to excel in specific disciplines, cultivating deeper engagement and critical thinking. In the primary years, this is about building the blocks so that pupils can be prepared for secondary school. This is also about being deliberate and explicit about the subject disciplines so that all pupils can thrive.

Here are some key benefits:

Critical thinking

Disciplinary literacy empowers pupils to read complex texts and information specific to each subject area. It encourages pupils to analyse, evaluate, and synthesise information from multiple sources, promoting deeper understanding and critical thinking skills.

Disciplinary literacy provides learners with the specialist vocabulary to understand and communicate in specific-subject areas. helps learners develop critical thinking and expertise in each subject, supporting their meta-cognition.

(Bedrock Learning, 2022)

Content area reading aims to build better students, and disciplinary literacy tries to get [learners] to grasp the ways literacy is used to create, disseminate, and critique information in the various disciplines.

(Professor Timothy Shanahan, 2019)

Communication skills

By mastering the language and conventions of different disciplines, pupils develop stronger communication skills, enabling them to express their ideas clearly and persuasively in both written and oral formats. As mentioned in this book, communication in the disciplines does not always have to be written. Pupils can use podcasts, performances and their digital skills etc. to show what they know.

It makes explicit the ways people within disciplinary communities think, read, and write. This allows students the opportunity to understand those practices so they can better navigate those spaces in society.

(Humphrey, 2024)

Disciplinary literacy is about teaching pupils the language they need to participate in a subject.

(Quigley et al, 2021a)

Engagement and motivation

Disciplinary literacy connects pupils to real-world applications of knowledge and skills, promoting a sense of relevance and purpose. This connection can spark greater interest and motivation in learning.

Therefore, the economic future of our state, as well as our students and their success as productive citizens and critical thinkers link to disciplinary literacy.

(Wisconsin Department of Public Instruction)

Appendix: Disciplinary literacy in other subjects

Disciplinary literacy can offer a powerful approach for schools to consider implementing in their school to improve equity of curriculum access.

(Quigley et al, 2021a)

Preparation for the future

By engaging in disciplinary literacy practices, pupils develop the skills and knowledge necessary for success in secondary education, higher education and future careers. They become adept at navigating the specific demands of different academic and professional fields.

One such benefit is that disciplinary literacy may be one of the most targeted ways to give students–especially historically marginalized ones–access to an exclusive space in society: academia.

(Humphrey, 2024)

An approach to improving literacy across the curriculum whereby all teachers are supported to understand how to teach students to read, write, and communicate effectively in their subject.

(Quigley et al, 2021a)

Connections across the curriculum

Disciplinary literacy encourages teachers to collaborate and integrate content across different subject areas. This approach helps pupils recognise the interconnectedness of knowledge and apply skills and concepts across disciplines.

Disciplinary literacy encourages teachers to collaborate and integrate content across subject areas.

(Wisconsin Department of Public Instruction)

In conclusion, disciplinary literacy offers a powerful approach to education, supports deeper comprehension, critical thinking, communication skills, engagement and preparation for future success. By embracing disciplinary literacy practices, teachers and leaders empower pupils to become active and informed participants in knowledge of the subject disciplines.

References

Butlin, C. (2023) EEF blog. Demystifying disciplinary literacy. A root and branch approach. https://educationendowmentfoundation.org.uk/news/demystifying-disciplinary-literacy-a-root-and-branch-approach (Accessed: 04/04/2025)

Davies, D. (2022) Disciplinary literacy. What is it and why is it important? Bedrock Learning [Blog] https://bedrocklearning.org/literacy-blogs/disciplinary-literacy/ (Accessed: 04/04/2025)

Humphrey, C. (2024) Disciplinary literacy and why is it important? Blog. Carnagie Learning. www.carnegielearning.com/blog/what-is-disciplinary-literacy/ (Accessed: 04/04/2025)

Quigley, A.& Coleman, R. (2021a) Improving Literacy in Secondary Schools: Guidance Report. Education Endowment Foundation. https://d2tic4wvo1iusb.cloudfront.net/production/eef-guidance-reports/literacy-ks3-ks4/EEF_KS3_KS4_LITERACY_GUIDANCE.pdf?v=1712491708 (Accessed: 04/04/2025)

Shanahan, T. (2019) Disciplinary Literacy in Primary Schools. https://ncca.ie/media/4679/disciplinary-literacy-in-the-primary-school-professor-timothy-shanahan-university-of-illinois-at-chicago-1.pdf (Accessed: 04/04/2025)

Wisconsin Department of Public Instruction. (2011) Common core state standards for literacy in All Subjects. https://dpi.wi.gov/sites/default/files/imce/cal/pdf/las-stds.pdf (Accessed: 04/04/2025)

Curriculum research bibliography

Alexander, R. (ed.) (2010) *Children, their World, their Education: Final Report and Recommendations of the Cambridge Primary Review*. Routledge.

Ali, L. (2000) The case for including black history in the national curriculum. *Improving School*, 3(1), 50–54.

Apple, M. (1993) The politics of official knowledge: Does a National Curriculum make sense? *Teachers College Records*, 95(2), 222–241.

Arthur, J. & Davison, J. (2000) Social literacy and citizenship in the school curriculum. *Curriculum Journal*, 11(1), 9–23.

Baer, J. (2003) The impact of the Core Knowledge curriculum on creativity. *Creativity Research Journal*, 15(2), 297–300.

Beard, R. (2008) *Primary Literacy: Research and Practice*. Institute of Education.

Bradley, R. (2005) Evaluation of the Core Knowledge program in Arkansas. www.coreknowledge.org/research (Accessed: 04/04/2025)

Chitty, C. (2004) *Education Policy in Britain*. Palgrave Limited.

Claxton, G. (2007) Expanding young people's capacity to learn. *British Journal of Educational Studies*, 55(2), 115–134.

Chambers, M. Powell, G. & Claxton, G. (2004) *Building 101 Ways to Learning Power*. TLO Limited.

Conway, D. (2010) *Liberal Education and the National Curriculum – Civitas*: Institute for the study of civil society. The Cromwell Press Group.

Exley, S. & Ball, S. (2011) Something old, something new… understanding Conservative education policy in Bochel, H. (ed.) *The Conservative Party and Social Policy*. Policy Press, 97–118.

Gathercole, S. & Pickering, S. J. (2001) Working memory deficits in children with low achievement in the national curriculum at 7 years. *British Journal of Educational Psychology*, 70, 177–194.

Goodson, I. (1992) On curriculum form: notes toward a theory of curriculum. *Sociology of Education*, 65(1), 66–75.

Green, S., Bell, J.F., Oates, T. & Bramley, T. (2008) Alternative approaches to National Curriculum assessment at KS1, KS2 and KS3. Cambridge

Assessment. www.cambridgeassessment.org.uk/ca/Our_Services/Research/Conference_Papers (Accessed: 04/04/2025)

Hargreaves, A. & Goodson, I. (2006) Educational change over time? The sustainability and non-sustainability of three decades of secondary school change and continuity. *Education Administration Quarterly*, 42(3), 3–41.

Hattie, J. (2009) *Visible Learning: A Synthesis of over 800 Meta-Analyses Relating to Achievement.* Routledge.

Higgins, S. Wall, K., Falzon, C., Hall, E. & Leat, D. (2005) *Learning to Learn in Schools: Phase 3 Evaluation Year 1 Final Report.* University of Newcastle: Centre for Learning and Teaching.

Hirsch, E.D. (2003) Reading comprehension requires knowledge of words and the world. American Federation of Teachers, 10–44. www.aft.org/sites/default/files/Hirsch.pdf (Accessed: 04/04/2025)

Hirsch, E.D. (2004) *The New First Dictionary of Cultural Literacy: What Your Child Needs to Know.* Houghton Mifflin Company.

Hirst, P. (2010) *Knowledge and the Curriculum: A Collection of Philosophical Papers.* Routledge and Kegan Paul.

Hoskins, B. & Fredriksson, U. (2008) Learning to learn: what is it and can it be measured? Centre for Research on Lifelong Learning http://publications.jrc.ec.europa.eu/repository/handle/111111111/979 (Accessed: 04/04/2025)

Johnson, M., Janisch, C. & Morgan-Fleming, B. (2001) Cultural literacy in classroom settings: teachers and students adapt the core knowledge curriculum. *Journal of Curriculum and Supervision*, 16(3), 259–272.

Johnson, M. (2007) *Subject to Change: New Thinking on the Curriculum.* Association of Teachers and Lecturers.

Lawton, D. (1988) The National Curriculum since 1988: panacea or poisoned chalice? *Forum*, 50(3), 337–342.

Lumsden, E., Mcbryde-Wilding, H. & Rose, H. (2010) Collaborative practice in enhancing the first-year student experience in Higher Education. *Enhancing the Learner in Higher Education*, 2(1), 12–21.

McHugh, B. & Stringfield, S. (1999) *Core Knowledge Curriculum: Three-Year Analysis of Implementation and Effects of Five Schools.* Department for Education: Center for Research on the Education of Students Placed at Risk.

Oates, T. (2010) *Could do Better: Using International Comparison to Refine the National Curriculum in England*. Cambridge Assessment.

Oates, T. (2002) Key Skills/Key Competencies: Avoiding the Pitfalls of Current Initiatives in Rychen, D., Salgarik, L. & McLaughlin, M. (eds) *Contributions to the second DeSe Co Symposium*. Swiss Federal Statistical Office.

Orwin, C. & Forbes, H.D. (1994) Cultural literacy: a Canadian perspective. *International Journal of Social Education*, 9(1), 15–30.

Partington, G. (1985) Multiculturalism and the common curriculum debate. *Society for Educational Studies*, 33(1), 35–56.

Paul, R.W. (1990) Critical and cultural literacy: where E.D. Hirsch goes wrong, in Paul, R.W. & Binker, A. (eds) Critical thinking: what every person needs to survive in a rapidly changing world. Centre for Critical Thinking and Moral Critique, Sonoma State University, 429–435.

Rawlings, E. (2001) The politics and practicalities of curriculum change 1991–2001 arising from a study of geography in England. *British Journal of Educational Studies*, 49(2), 137–158.

Ruddock, G. & Sainsbury, M. (2008) *Comparison of the Core Primary Curriculum in England to those of Other High Performing Countries*. National Foundation for Educational Research and DCSF publications.

Stobart, G. (2008) *Testing Times*. Routledge Publications.

Trilling, B. & Fadel, C. (2009) 21st Century Skills: Learning for Life in our Times. Jossey-Bass Publications.

Vail, K. (1997) Core comes to Crooksville. *American School Board Journal*, 184(3), 14–18.

Wedman, J. & Waigandt, A. (2004) Core Knowledge curriculum and school performance: A National Study www.coreknowledge.org/research. (Accessed: 04/04/2025)

Wiliam, D. (1996) National curriculum assessments and programmes of study: validity and impact. *British Educational Research Journal*, 22(1), 129–141.

Acronyms and abbreviations

DfE – UK Department for Education

Ofsted – UK Office for Standards in Education, Children's Services and Skills.

EYFS – Early Years Foundation Stage. This covers children from birth to five years old. This book focusses on pupils in nursery and reception (aged 3–5 years old).

KS1 – Key stage 1. Pupils are aged 5–7 years old.

KS2 – Key stage 2. Pupils are 7–11 years old.

Primary – pupils are 5–11 years old in England.